Copyright © 2025 by Lewis Mabee

All rights reserved. No part of this book may be reproduced, stored in a retrieval system, or transmitted in any form or by any means — electronic, mechanical, photocopying, recording, or otherwise — without prior written permission of the author, except in the case of brief quotations used in reviews or articles.

ISBN: 978-1-0696649-8-3 (Paperback Edition)

This book is a work of humor. Names, characters, events, and scenarios are products of the author's imagination and are used for comedic purposes only. Any resemblance to real persons, living or dead, or actual events is purely coincidental (though if your date once arrived on stilts carrying narwhal balloons, please know you are our hero).

Published by The Lewis Mabee Group

First Edition: 2025

Table of Contents

Introduction 4

What's Inside the Book & How to Use It 5

A Message from the Author 6

Chapter 1 – Grand Entrances, Terrible Impressions 7

Chapter 2 – The Walk of Weirdness 18

Chapter 3 – Icebreakers That Shatter the Ice 29

Chapter 4 – The Date Activity Nobody Asked For 40

Chapter 5 – Competitive Chaos 51

Chapter 6 – Oversharing, Overhearing, Over It 62

Chapter 7 – Snack Break from Hell 73

Chapter 8 – The Universe Interrupts 84

Chapter 9 – The Desperate Recovery Attempt 95

Chapter 10 – The Big WTF Moment 106

Chapter 11 – The Awkward Goodbye Nobody Wanted 117

Chapter 12 – The Ride Home Disaster Parade 128

Reader's Challenge 139

Final Laugh 139

Acknowledgments 139

Keep the Book Going by Sharing 140

A Thank You Note from Lewis 140

About the Author 140

Introduction

Dating has never been normal. It's awkward, unpredictable, and occasionally feels like the universe is running a hidden camera show just for you. That's precisely why this book exists.

Inside, you'll find scenarios that no sane person would actually wish for on a date — but if life has taught us anything, it's that sanity rarely shows up when romance does. You won't find candlelit dinners and polite small talk here. Instead, you'll crash through dates where mimes, aliens, malfunctioning props, and giant sandwiches all want their moment to shine.

Each page dares you to choose between two catastrophes, then adds reflections, odd trivia, and a chance to laugh about what dating already feels like sometimes: absurd theatre with bad lighting.

This isn't a book of advice. It's a book of escape, exaggeration, and entertainment. Whether you're single, taken, or still recovering from your last "what just happened?" night out, these pages are here to remind you that no matter how messy your love life gets, at least you weren't dropped home in a fish tank or mistaken for a time traveler (probably).

So, grab a friend, a date, or even your cat, and dive in. Pick sides. Argue about the worst options. Share your answers. And most of all, laugh — because if dating teaches us anything, it's that sometimes, you either laugh about it or cry into your breadsticks.

Welcome to the worst first dates you'll never have — unless the universe really hates you.

What's Inside the Book & How to Use It

This isn't just a book. It's a dumpster fire of first-date scenarios that got loose and demanded page space. Inside, you'll stumble into:

- Questions that make you wonder if romance is worth it.
- Reflections that add zero wisdom but plenty of snark.
- Fun facts that are weirdly true, which feels illegal in a book this dumb.
- Share It prompts are designed to ruin friendships and make strangers question your sanity online.

Now, before you go full chaos gremlin, a few "guidelines" (read: survival tactics)

- Pick a question.
- Debate it with friends, strangers, or unlucky dates.
- Argue until someone cries, storms out, or admits they'd rather be catapulted home in a deli sub.
- If you survive, repeat.

Basically, flip a page, laugh until your abs hurt (or until a waiter questions you about why you're crying into your soup), and then scream your answers at whoever's closest. Bonus points if it's an unsuspecting Uber driver.

And if you're brave enough to broadcast your choices to the world, don't forget to tag #FirstDateWYR — because misery, chaos, and second-hand embarrassment all love company.

Disclaimer (The "Don't Try This at Home" Part)

This book is pure comedy. If you actually attempt any of this — like commuting home on a conveyor belt, proposing via skywriter by accident, or being chauffeured by a talking snail — you're beyond help, and that's between you, your insurance company, and possibly the fire department.

Any resemblance to real people, places, or events is purely coincidental (though if you've ever been serenaded mid-bite by a gospel choir screaming breakup songs, we owe you royalties — but only in coupons).

And yes, the hashtag again: #FirstDateWYR. Because if you're going down in flames, at least let the internet roast you properly.

A Message from the Author

First dates are terrifying. Trust me, I've been on enough of them to know it only takes about three minutes to figure out whether it's going to be a romantic evening or a disaster you'll never forget. Was it the awkward hug-or-handshake moment? Or was it the second I asked myself, "Should I really have ordered appetizers?"

This book was born out of those very moments—the kind that make you want to crawl under the table, but later become the stories your friends demand you retell. I started collecting every ridiculous scenario I could imagine and thought, why not turn them into a game? Because if we're all going to suffer through first dates, we might as well laugh about it together.

So here it is: 120 absurd, over-the-top Would You Rather questions designed to take the edge off dating, friendship, parties, or even just a lonely Tuesday night when you want to feel grateful you're not actually trapped in one of these situations.

If this book makes you laugh out loud, choke on your drink, or question humanity just a little, then I've done my job. Thanks for taking it home—you've officially made my awkwardness worth it. Now go find someone you trust enough to laugh with… or torture with these questions.

—Lewis Mabee

Chapter 1 – Grand Entrances, Terrible Impressions

Vibe: Over-the-top arrivals and awkward first moments that scream "this is already a mistake."

The second you show up, it's clear Cupid called in sick.

Would you Rather...

Show up 15 minutes early to the zoo and get mistaken for the new ostrich wrangler,

or

15 minutes late carrying a half-eaten funnel cake the size of a steering wheel?

Reflection
Early bird gets pecked, late bird gets powdered sugar tattoos before hello.

Share It
Which disaster screams "dating material" louder — ostrich chaos or funnel cake shame? #FirstDateWYR

Fun Fact
Ostriches can sprint up to 70 km/h, making them the fastest two-legged animal on Earth.

Would you Rather...

Spill your iced latte on yourself at the cat café,

or

dramatically pour it on your date like you're auditioning for a feline soap opera?

Reflection
One makes you clumsy, the other makes you the villain in a show cats already hated.

Share It
Which one gets you blacklisted from every cat café in town?
#FirstDateWYR

Fun Fact
The world's first cat café opened in Taipei, Taiwan, in 1998.

Would you Rather...

Trip over your own feet entering the roller rink,

or

panic and moonwalk the entire way across the glowing floor?

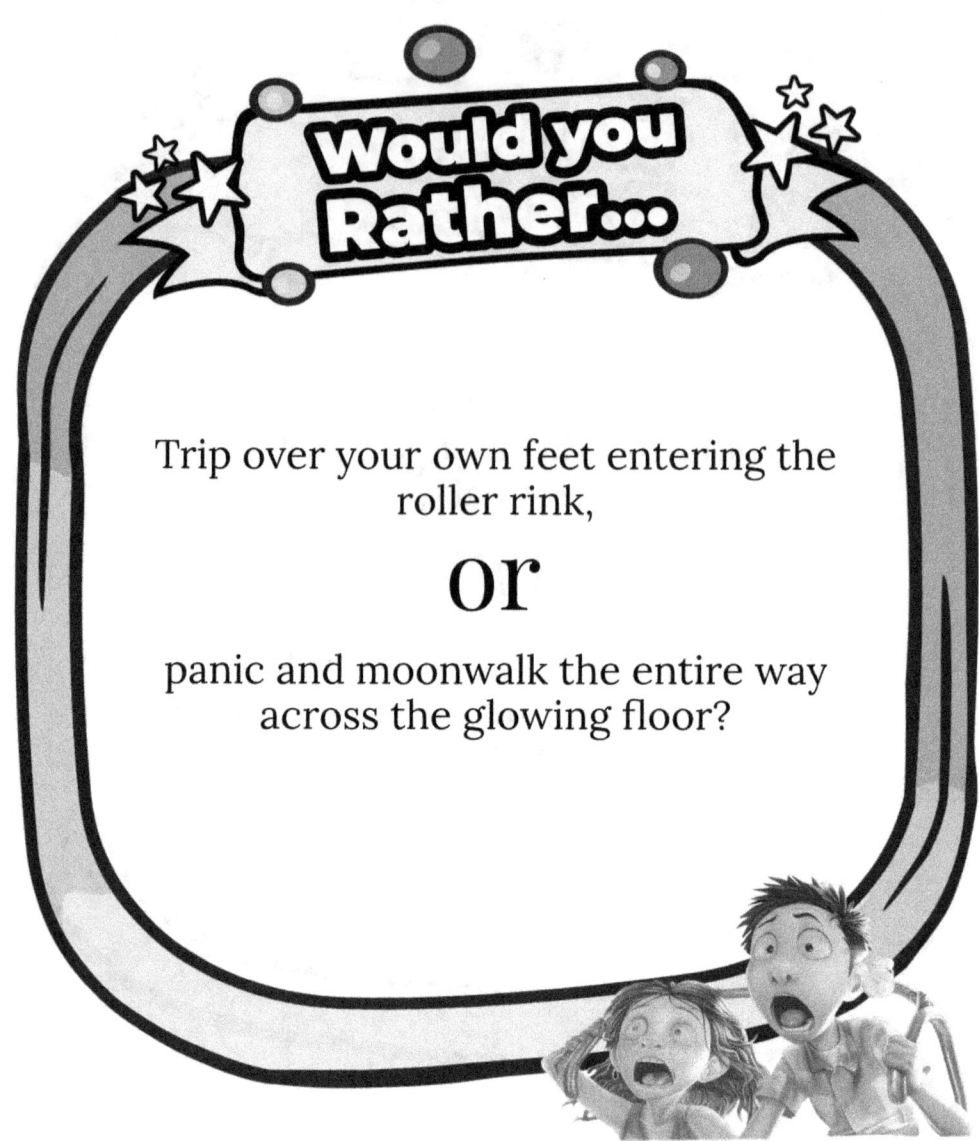

Reflection
One's a quick splat, the other's a 20-meter slow-motion humiliation reel.

Share It
Who's stopping the DJ first — the paramedics or the crowd demanding an encore? #FirstDateWYR

Fun Fact
Roller disco peaked in the 1970s, combining skating with dance club vibes.

Would you Rather...

Call your date by your ex's name in the art museum,

or

loudly introduce them as "The Future Mr./Mrs. Please-Don't-Be-a-Felon" while tourists stare?

Reflection
One's intimate sabotage, the other's a public service announcement gone wrong.

Share It
Which mistake lands you in the museum gift shop crying into a snow globe? #FirstDateWYR

Fun Fact
The Louvre is the most visited museum in the world, hosting over 9 million guests annually.

Would you Rather...

Sneeze so hard mid-handshake at the aquarium that you headbutt the stingray tank,

or

greet your date with jazz hands under the dolphin show spotlight?

Reflection
One's an ER bill, the other's a Broadway debut you didn't rehearse.

Share It
Which one becomes a TikTok thirst trap for the wrong reasons? #FirstDateWYR

Fun Fact
Dolphins are one of the few non-human species proven to recognize themselves in mirrors.

Would you Rather...

Arrive wearing clown shoes at the outdoor food truck festival,

or

show up in a full wedding dress at the farmer's market?

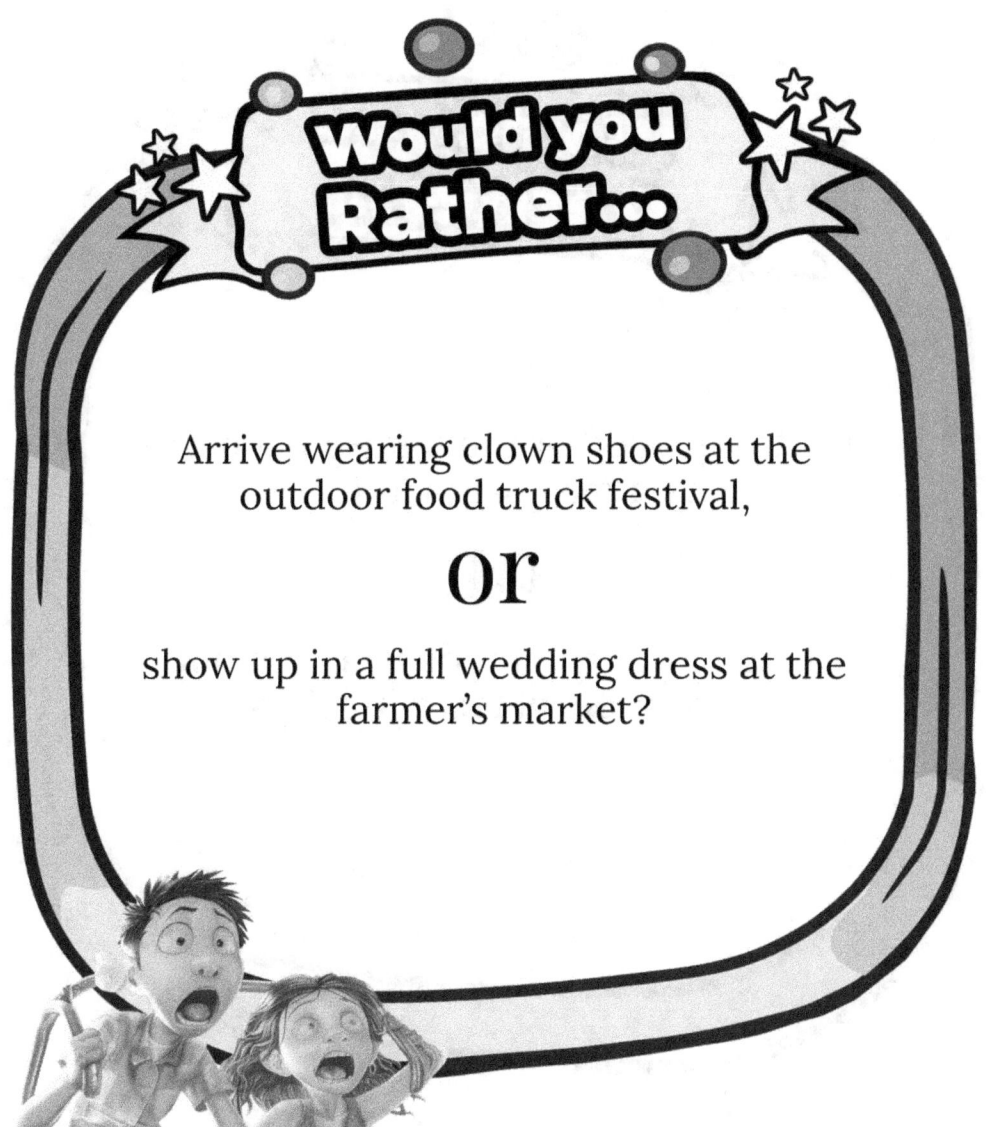

Reflection
Either you're honking for tacos or sampling bridal cake too early.

Share It
Which one gets you offered free therapy by strangers?
#FirstDateWYR

Fun Fact
The Guinness World Record for the largest food truck rally included 121 trucks in Tampa, Florida.

Would you Rather...

Be dropped off at the mini-golf course by a mall Santa in July,

or

carried into the arcade in a hammock by four bewildered jugglers?

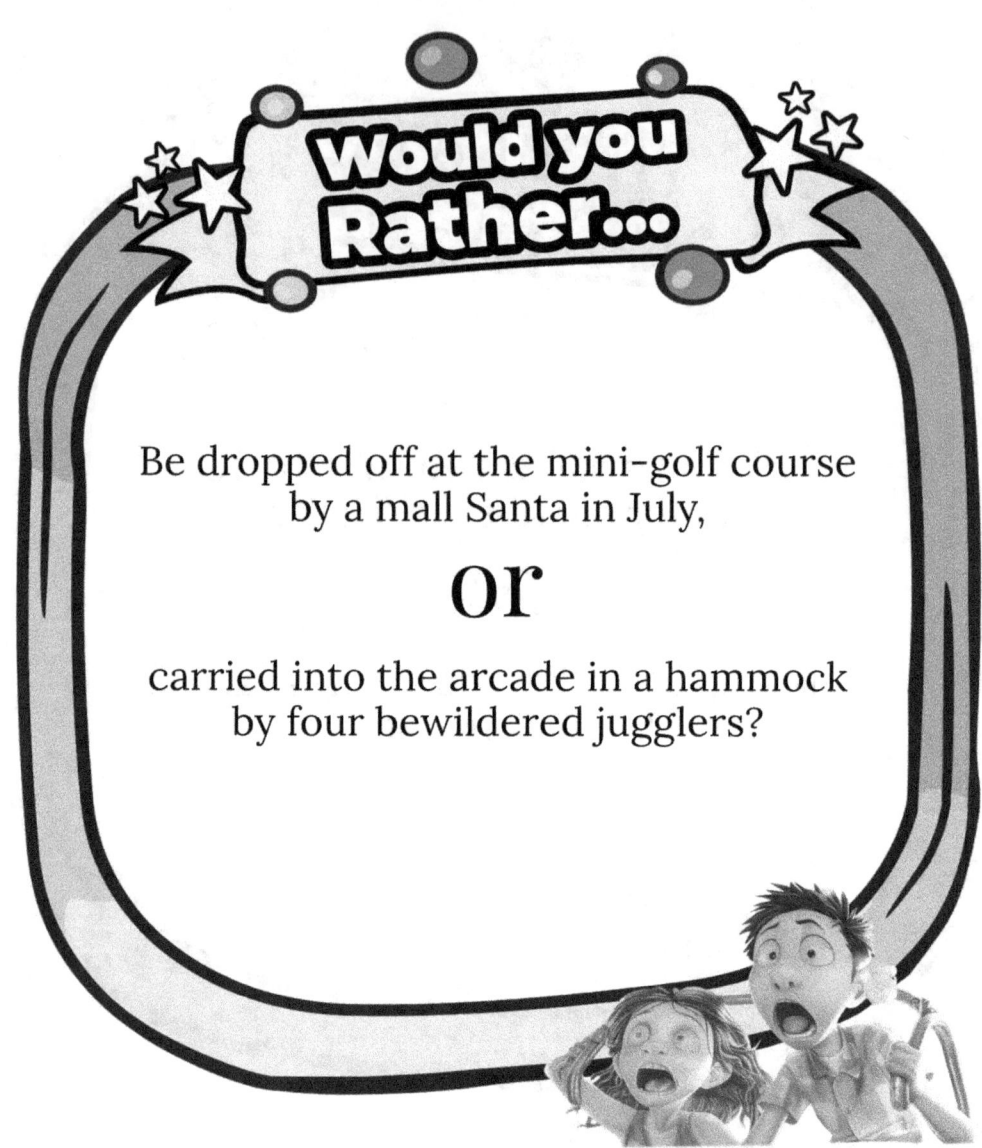

Reflection
One is off-season trauma, the other is Cirque du Nope.

Share It
Who's more confused — your date or the kids crying in line for tokens? #FirstDateWYR

Fun Fact
The first official miniature golf course opened in 1916 in North Carolina.

Would you Rather...

Arrive on stilts so tall you can't fit into the bowling alley,

or

ride in on a runaway bumper car that won't shut off in the parking lot?

Reflection
You're either skyscraper awkward or demolition derby chic.

Share It
Which entrance gets you trending under #PublicMenace first? #FirstDateWYR

Fun Fact
The fastest recorded bowling ball throw was clocked at over 100 km/h.

Grand Entrances, Terrible Impressions

Would you Rather...

Ride into the park picnic on an electric scooter stacked with 12 flamingo lawn ornaments,

or

skateboard down the boardwalk holding helium balloons shaped like pufferfish?

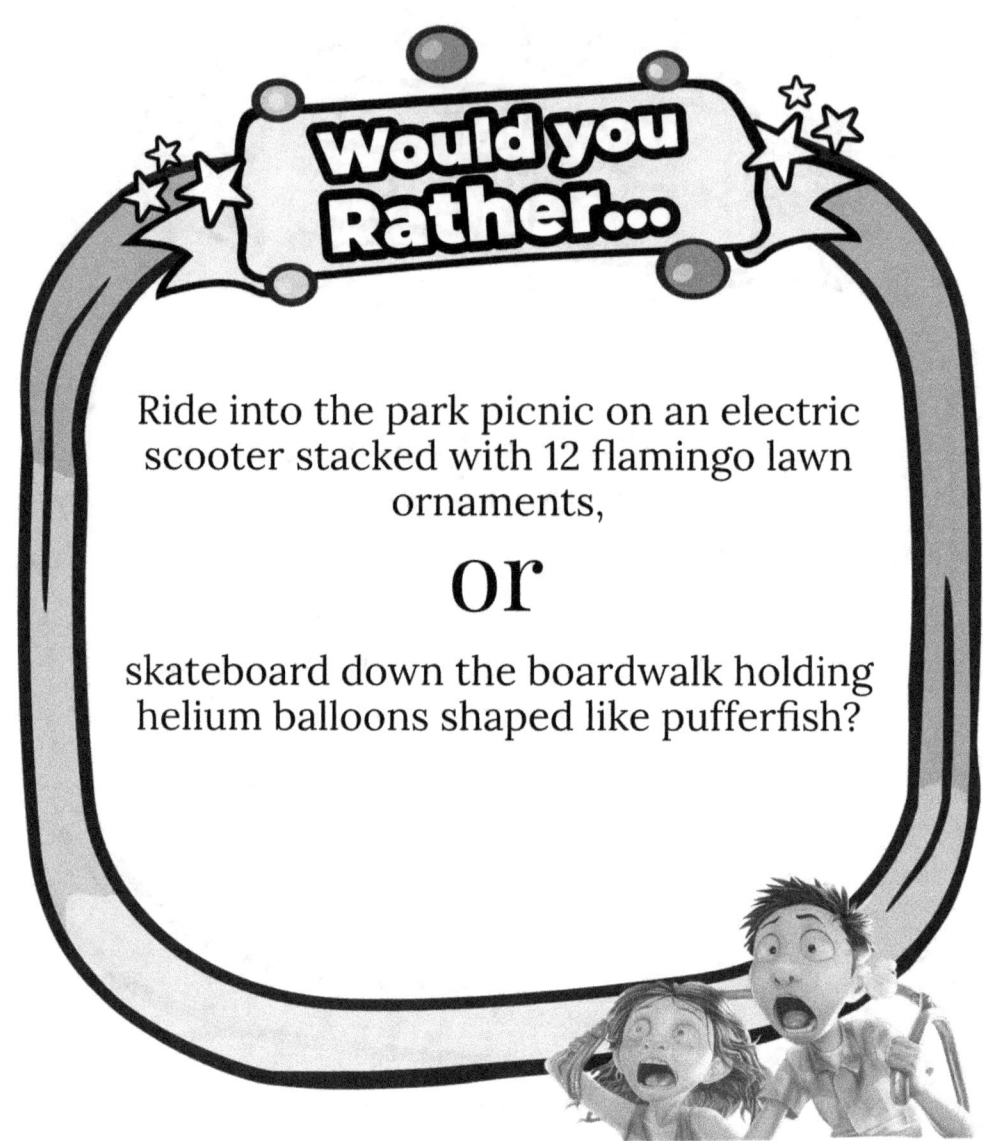

Reflection
One's a suburban fever dream, the other's pure carnival nightmare.

Share It
Who's calling security faster — a lifeguard or a jealous gardener? #FirstDateWYR

Fun Fact
Pink flamingo lawn ornaments were first sold in 1957 and became a kitschy American icon.

Would you Rather...

Be escorted into the ice rink by a kazoo marching band,

or

bounce in on a pogo stick while balancing a sombrero full of nachos?

Reflection
One is sonic torture, the other is gravity's cruel joke.

Share It
Which one would you actually tell your grandkids without lying? #FirstDateWYR

Fun Fact
The pogo stick was patented in Germany in 1920.

Grand Entrances, Terrible Impressions

Chapter 2 – The Walk of Weirdness

***Vibe:** The journey to the date spot gets hijacked by bizarre encounters, props, and public humiliation.*

You haven't even arrived yet, and the universe is already begging you to turn back.

Would you Rather...

Walk past a brass band that insists on following you while playing the same three notes,

or

get trailed by a tour bus group convinced you're their celebrity lookalike?

Reflection
Either way, your date is now starring in a parade they didn't buy tickets for.

Share It
Who's more likely to dump you mid-walk — your date or the trombone section? #FirstDateWYR

Fun Fact
A trombone can hit over 110 decibels, nearly as loud as a jet taking off.

Would you Rather...

Cut through a reptile petting zoo and get chased by an escaped iguana,

or

wander into a dog park where 40 golden retrievers bolt straight at you?

Reflection
One's a lizard chase scene, the other's a stampede of golden chaos.

Share It
Which animal ambush gets you trending under #DateFails first? #FirstDateWYR

Fun Fact
Iguanas can fall 50 feet from trees and survive — sometimes knocking people out on impact.

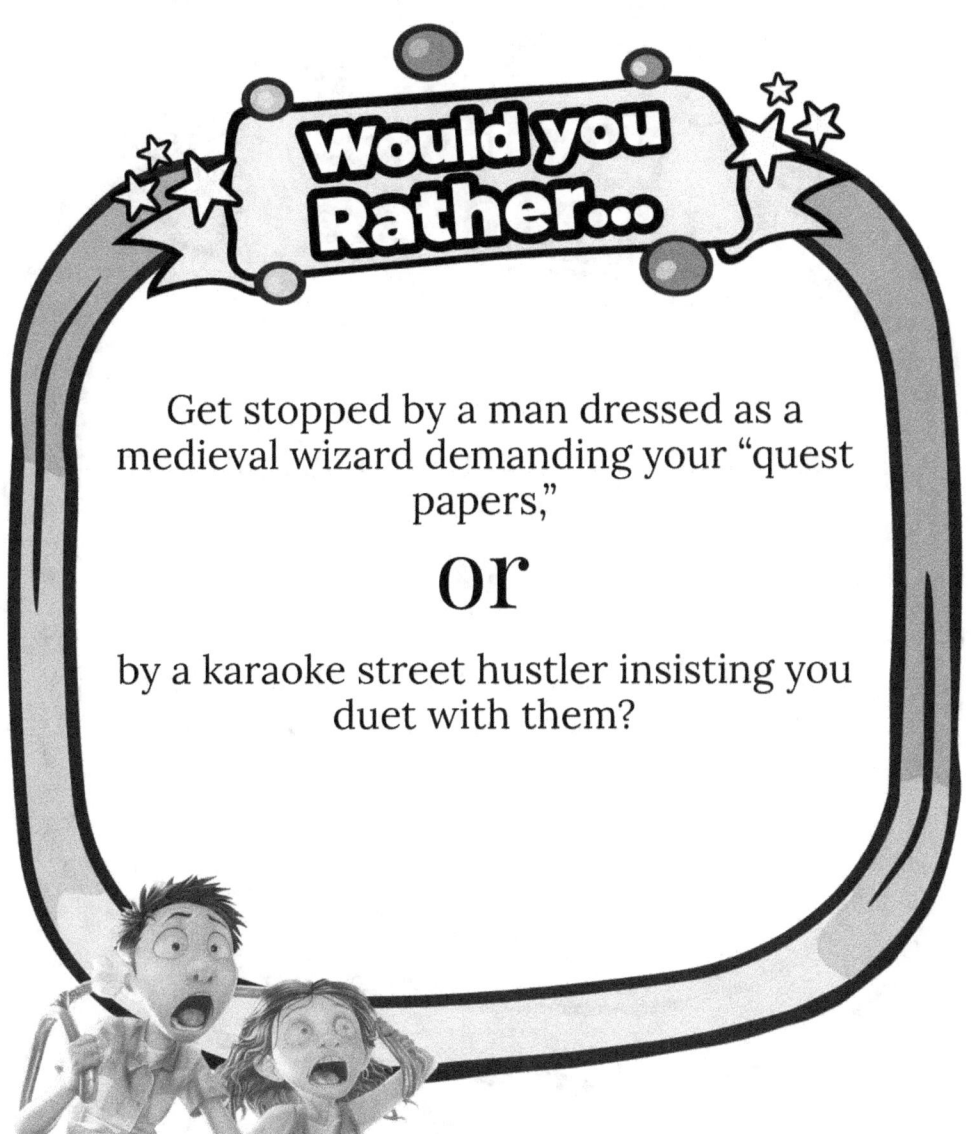

Would you Rather...

Get stopped by a man dressed as a medieval wizard demanding your "quest papers,"

or

by a karaoke street hustler insisting you duet with them?

Reflection
One's Dungeons & Dragons, the other's American Idol gone wrong.

Share It
Which ambush ruins your dignity faster — fake wizardry or off-key Whitney Houston? #FirstDateWYR

Fun Fact
Karaoke originated in Japan in the 1970s and translates to "empty orchestra."

Would you Rather...

Pass through a flash mob of interpretive dance dressed as giant fruit,

or

through a medieval battle reenactment that ropes you in as "unarmed peasant #4"?

Reflection
You thought it was coffee, now it's community theatre.

Share It
Who's filming you first — the TikTok crowd or the knight with a GoPro on his helmet?
#FirstDateWYR

Fun Fact
The largest flash mob had over 38,000 people in the Philippines in 2009.

Would you Rather...

Take a shortcut through a farmers' market and knock over a 12-foot tower of cheese wheels,

or

bump into someone juggling chainsaws "for tips"?

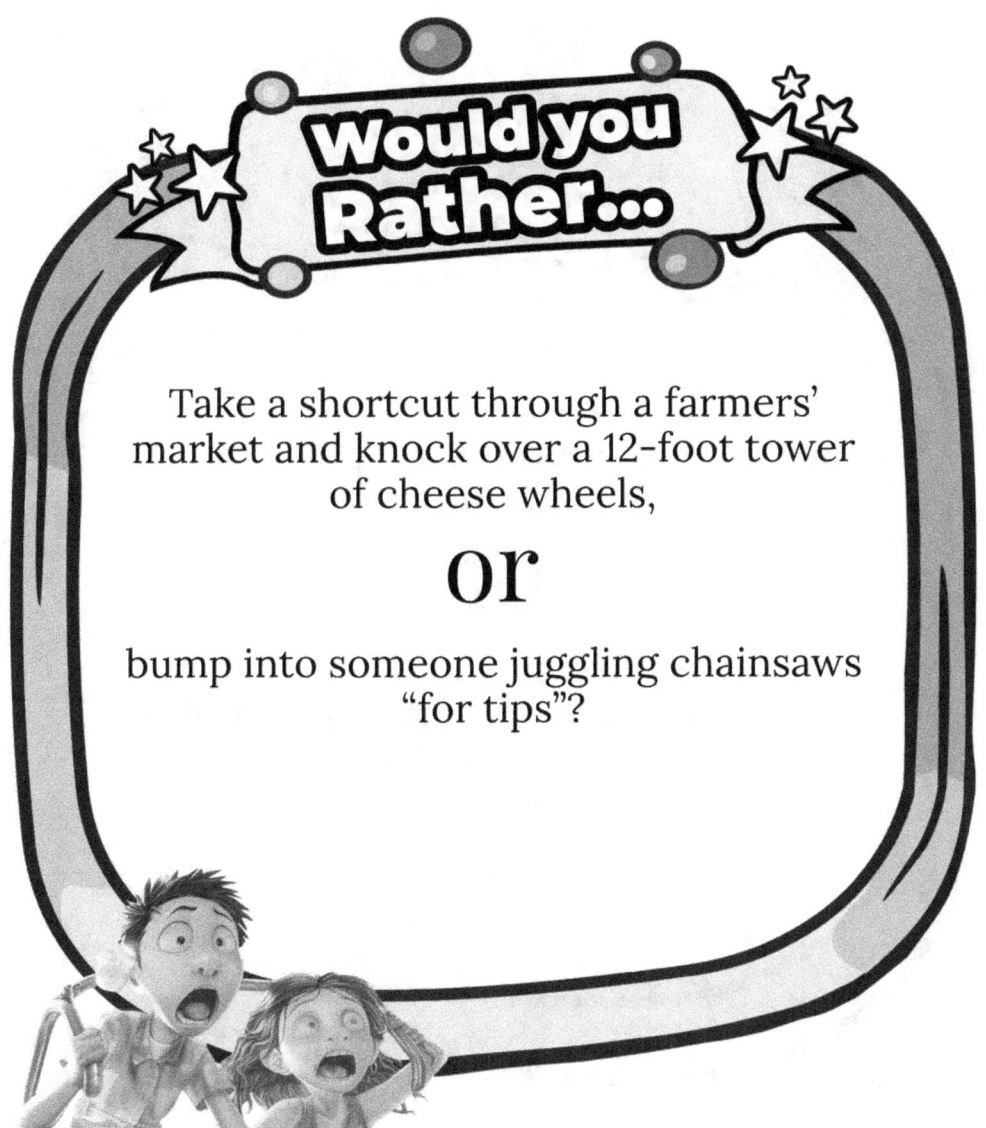

Reflection
One's dairy doom, the other's an ER bill waiting to happen.

Share It
Which disaster snack gets you famous on local news? #FirstDateWYR

Fun Fact
The world's biggest cheese wheel weighed over 20,000 pounds and was made in Canada.

Would you Rather...

Be forced to detour through a swamp full of mosquitos,

or

through a construction site where you're handed a jackhammer as "safety equipment"?

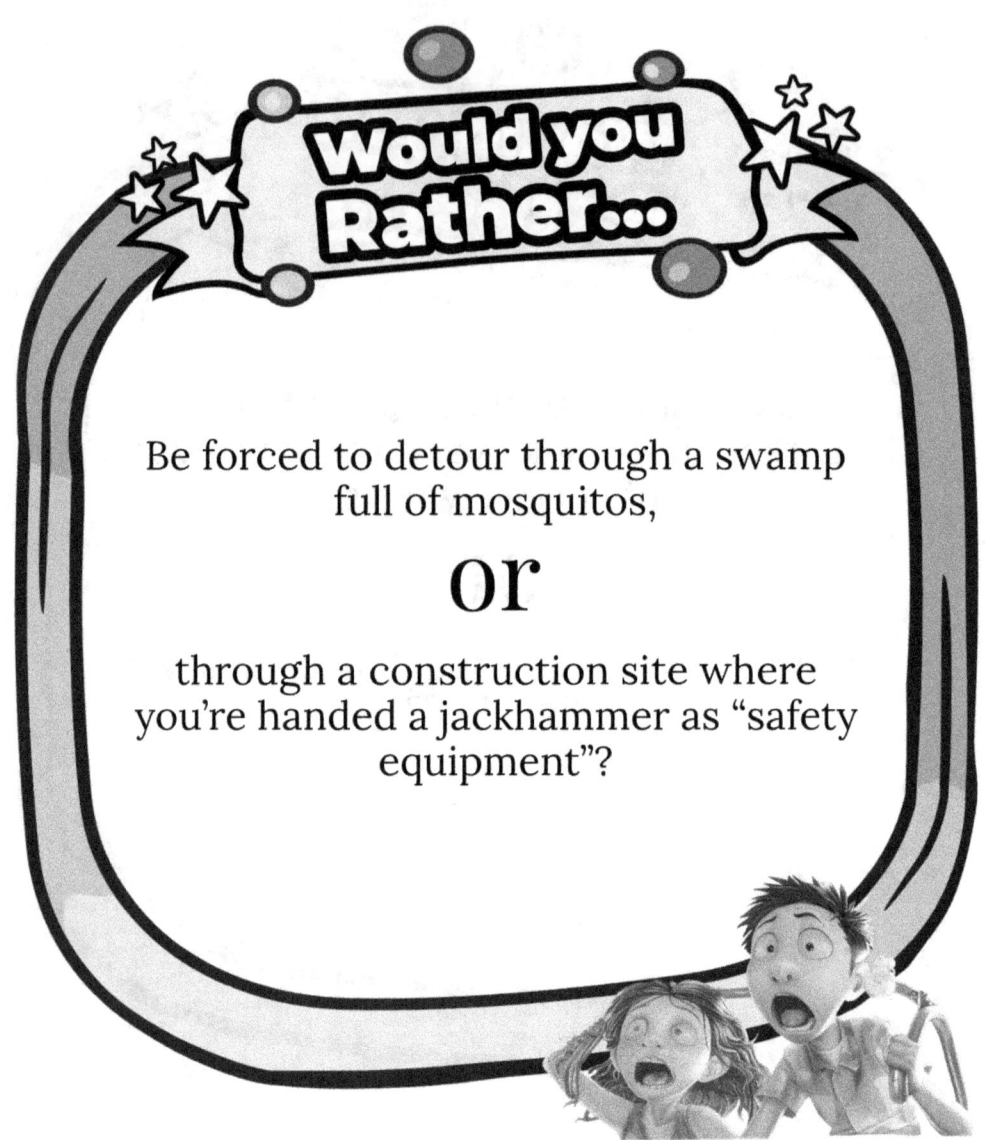

Reflection
Either way, you look like you're on parole, not a date.

Share It
Which one screams romance louder — bug bites or worker's comp paperwork? #FirstDateWYR

Fun Fact
Mosquitos are attracted to carbon dioxide, body heat, and even certain perfumes.

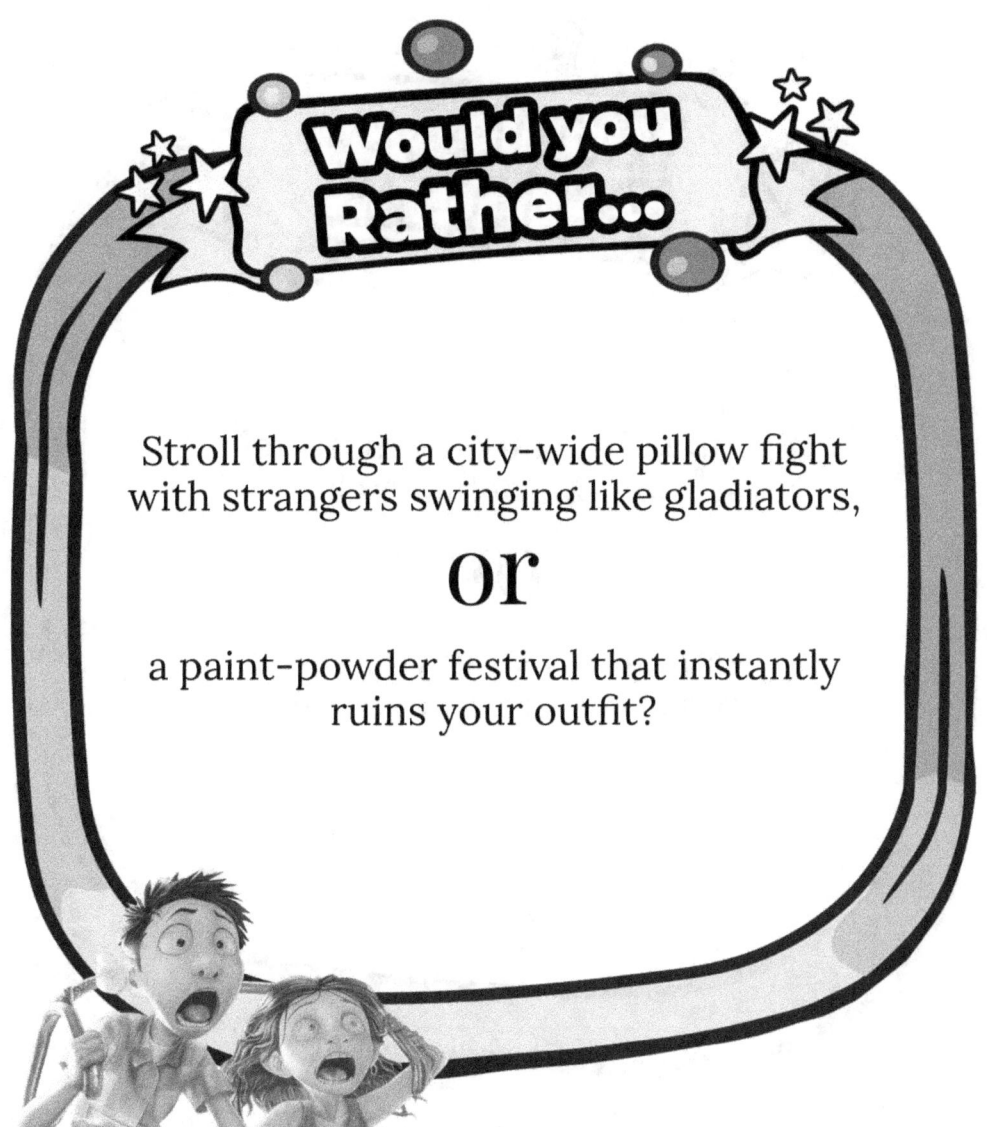

Would you Rather...

Stroll through a city-wide pillow fight with strangers swinging like gladiators,

or

a paint-powder festival that instantly ruins your outfit?

Reflection
One is feathers in your mouth, the other is rainbow laundry doom.

Share It
Who's filing for dry-cleaning damages first — you or your date? #FirstDateWYR

Fun Fact
The Indian festival Holi inspired many modern paint-powder events worldwide.

The Walk of Weirdness

Would you Rather...

Get stopped by a guy trying to sell you a raccoon out of his backpack,

or

a woman insisting you adopt a miniature pig immediately?

Reflection
Forget dinner — you're now parents.

Share It
Which questionable pet would you take home and regret instantly? #FirstDateWYR

Fun Fact
Mini pigs can weigh up to 150 pounds when fully grown, despite the "mini" name.

Would you Rather...

Accidentally join a protest march chanting slogans you don't understand,

or

get swept into a marathon where people hand you energy gels?

Reflection
One's activism cosplay, the other's cardio torture.

Share It
Which one ruins your date shoes faster — angry chanting or runner's blisters? #FirstDateWYR

Fun Fact
The modern marathon distance (42.195 km) was standardized at the 1908 London Olympics.

The Walk of Weirdness

Would you Rather...

Take a "romantic" shortcut through an abandoned mall fountain filled with questionable rainwater,

or

across a frozen rink with no skates and 200 kids zooming past?

Reflection
Slipping and screaming: the ultimate flirting technique.

Share It
Who's more likely to call 911 — you, your date, or the rink manager? #FirstDateWYR

Fun Fact
At their peak, the U.S. had over 1,500 shopping malls; many are now abandoned relics.

Chapter 3 – Icebreakers That Shatter the Ice

Vibe: Small talk goes wildly off course — instead of "what do you do for work?" it's "why are you holding that taxidermied seahorse?"

Any chance of a normal conversation has already drowned in absurdity.

Would you Rather...

Talk about your childhood while standing under a malfunctioning fountain spraying sideways,

or

while trapped inside a bouncy castle with 12 toddlers in sugar-rush mode?

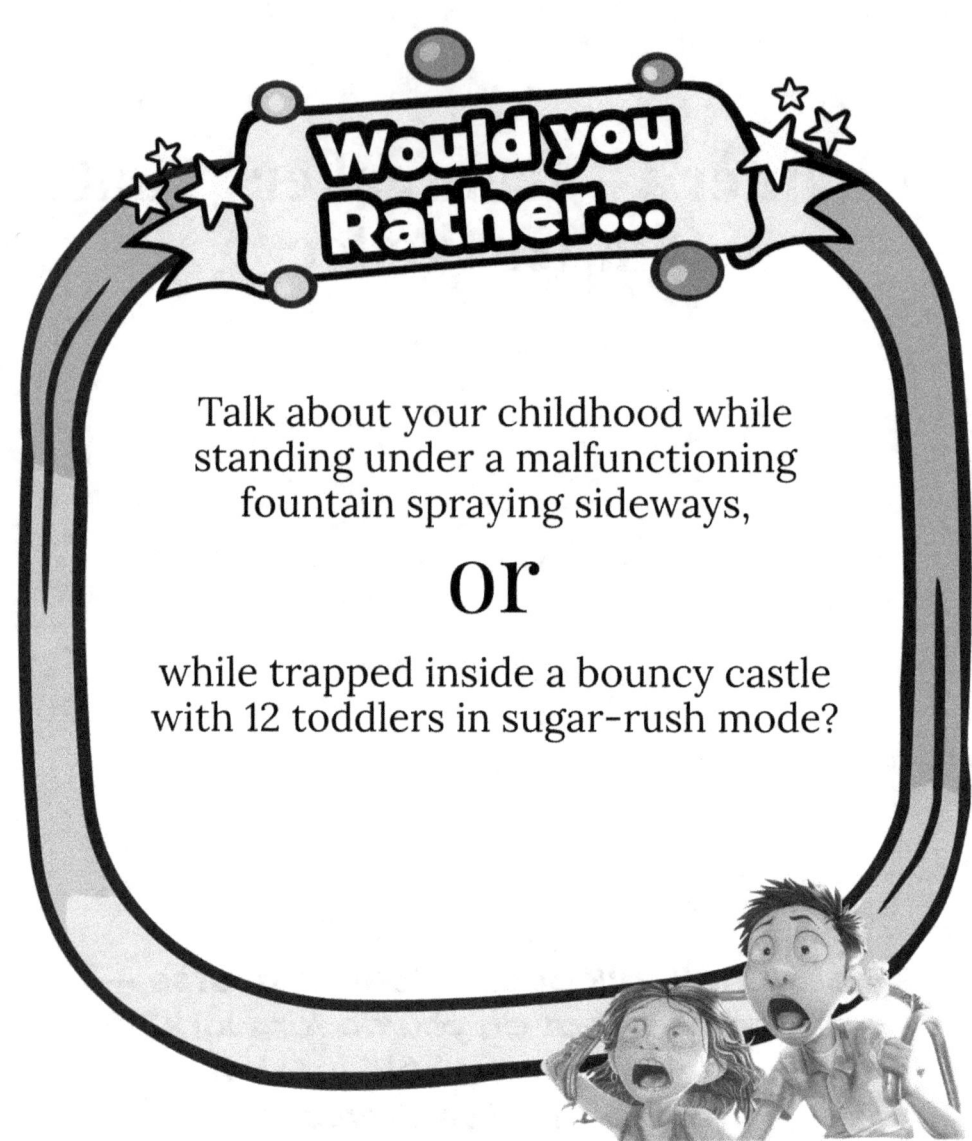

Reflection
Either way, trauma bonding comes with wet socks or bruised ribs.

Share It
Which cursed setting makes "So where did you grow up?" feel like a hostage situation? #FirstDateWYR

Fun Fact
The world's largest bounce house is over 25,000 square feet.

Would you Rather...

Learn about their hobbies while sitting beside a man practicing the tuba,

or

in front of a unicyclist juggling flaming batons?

Reflection
Your date's life story is competing with either bass blasts or a circus fire hazard.

Share It
Which background act would you rage-quit flirting through first? #FirstDateWYR

Fun Fact
The tuba is the lowest-pitched brass instrument, invented in 1835.

Would you Rather...

Have your "What do you do for work?" interrupted by a clown staging a fake hostage scene,

or

by a child with a vuvuzela solo?

Reflection
One is theatre of nightmares, the other is pure sonic warfare.

Share It
Which interruption would make you delete your dating apps on the spot? #FirstDateWYR

Fun Fact
Vuvuzelas gained global fame during the 2010 FIFA World Cup in South Africa.

Would you Rather...

Reveal your favorite movies while a street preacher yells about aliens,

or

while a barbershop quartet follows you singing "I Will Always Love You"?

Reflection
Subtle conversation is impossible; awkward serenades are forever.

Share It
Which vibe ruins romance harder — UFO panic or boy-band ballads?
#FirstDateWYR

Fun Fact
The first commercial barbershop quartet recordings were made in the 1890s.

Would you Rather...

Ask about family while a roaming seagull dive-bombs your fries,

or

while a goat tries to eat your shoe?

Reflection
One steals your snacks, the other steals your dignity.

Share It
Which animal sidekick would wreck your family story faster? #FirstDateWYR

Fun Fact
Seagulls have learned to imitate human actions, like opening chip bags.

Would you Rather...

Share your vacation memory while a street artist insists on drawing you badly,

or

while a caricaturist gives you a forehead the size of a billboard?

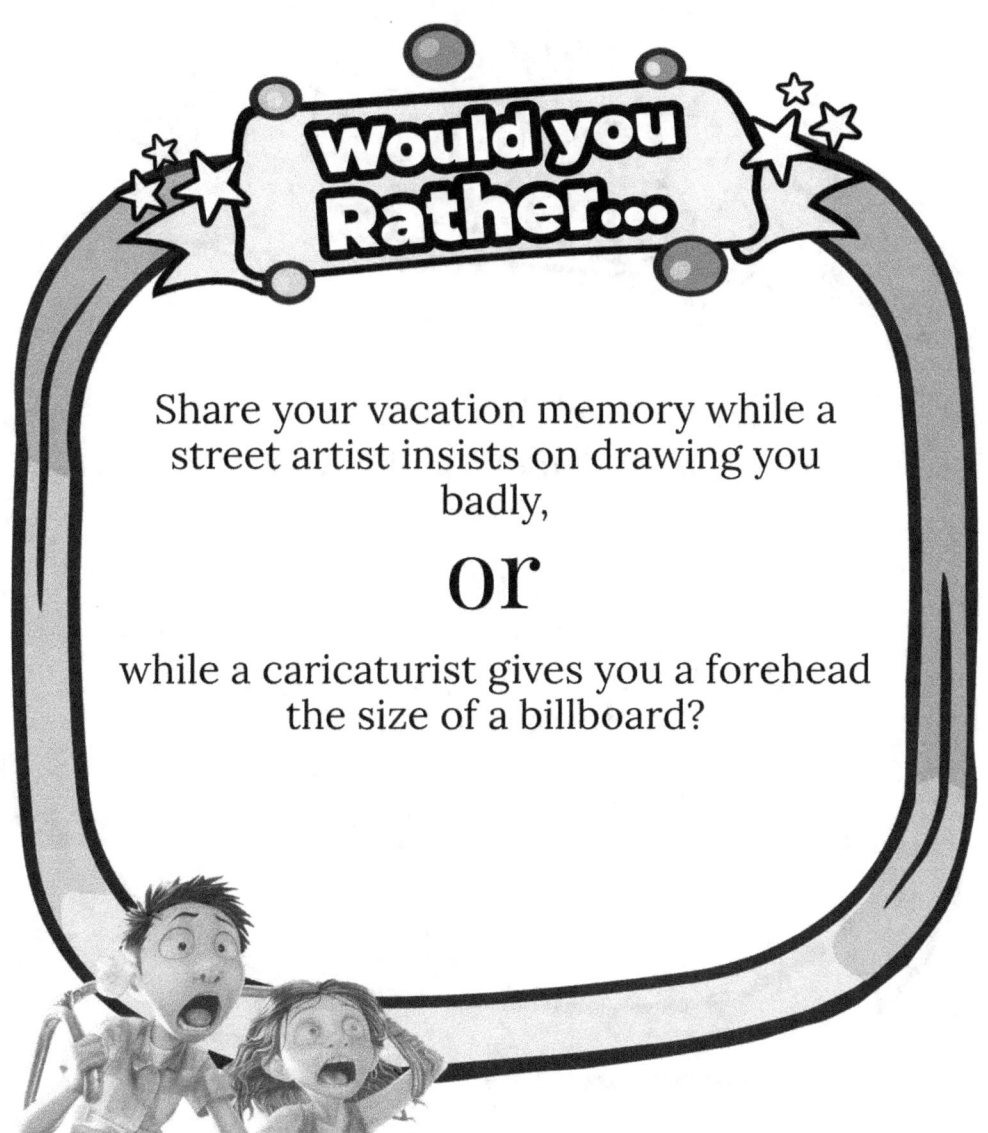

Reflection
Nothing kills nostalgia faster than cartoon humiliation.

Share It
Which "art" would you rip up first before posting online? #FirstDateWYR

Fun Fact
Leonardo da Vinci sketched caricature-like faces over 500 years ago.

Would you Rather...

Talk about childhood pets while someone in a giant pickle costume waves,

or

while a magician keeps asking to saw your date in half?

Reflection
Either way, your pet story is overshadowed by fermented vegetables or fake murder.

Share It
Which third wheel ruins the vibe faster — Giant Pickle or Budget Houdini? #FirstDateWYR

Fun Fact
The world's largest recorded pickle weighed over 9 pounds.

Would you Rather...

Discuss favorite foods while a brass street band blasts behind you,

or

while an ice cream truck loops its jingle for 45 minutes?

Reflection
You can't romance through either trumpets or trauma jingles.

Share It
Which soundtrack would haunt your dreams longer? #FirstDateWYR

Fun Fact
The first ice cream truck began operating in Ohio in 1920.

Would you Rather...

Reveal your favorite childhood TV show while a balloon artist forces balloon swords into your hands,

or

while a vendor aggressively tries to sell you counterfeit perfume?

Reflection
Nostalgia never stood a chance against balloon violence or eau de regret.

Share It
Which distraction makes you wish for subtitles mid-date? #FirstDateWYR

Fun Fact
Fake perfume seizures worldwide are worth billions annually.

Would you Rather...

Ask about their dream job while someone butchers karaoke nearby,

or

while a drunk man insists you hold his taxidermied squirrel?

Reflection
One ruins ambition with bad singing, the other with furry trauma.

Share It
Which one would make you text your group chat "pick me up NOW"? #FirstDateWYR

Fun Fact
Taxidermy has been practiced for centuries, with early examples traced back to ancient Egypt.

Chapter 4 – The Date Activity Nobody Asked For

Vibe: Forget dinner and drinks. These activities are unhinged, impractical, and socially unacceptable first-date choices.

What should be "fun" now looks like a rejected Fear Factor episode.

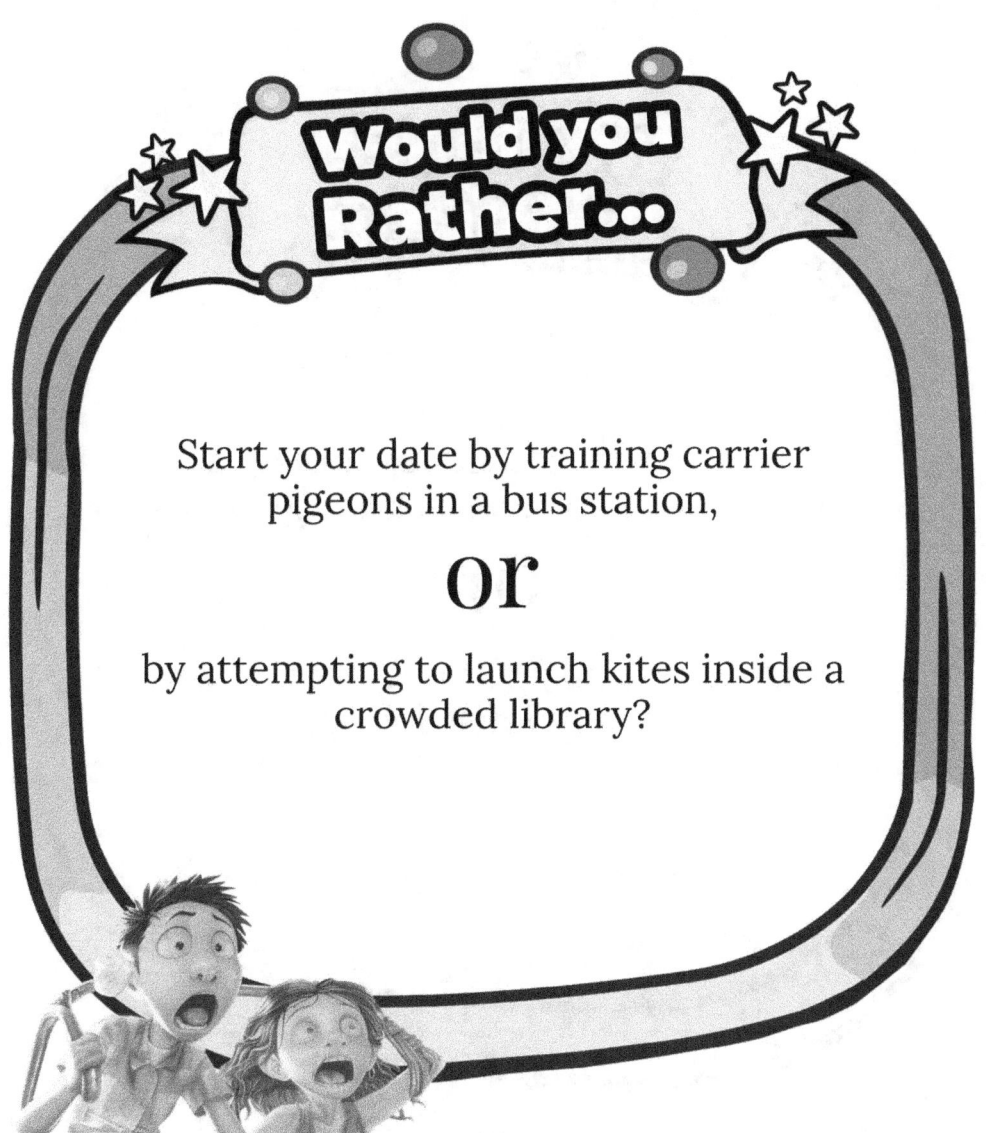

Would you Rather...

Start your date by training carrier pigeons in a bus station,

or

by attempting to launch kites inside a crowded library?

Reflection
Less romance, more eviction notice.

Share It
Which "hobby" gets you banned faster — pigeon poop or kite strings in the stacks?
#FirstDateWYR

Fun Fact
Carrier pigeons were used as military messengers as late as World War II.

The Date Activity Nobody Asked For

Would you Rather...

Begin your activity by joining a competitive cabbage-throwing contest,

or

a mashed potato sculpting showdown in a courthouse lobby?

Reflection
Vegetables weren't meant to be foreplay.

Share It
Which carb crime would land you on YouTube first? #FirstDateWYR

Fun Fact
Finland has a sport called "cabbage bowling," where competitors roll cabbages like bowling balls.

Would you Rather...

Kick off the date with underwater basket-weaving in a hotel pool,

or

a speed-knitting tournament in a sauna?

Reflection
Soggy yarn vs. sweaty yarn: no survivors.

Share It
Which craft fail would your grandkids laugh at first? #FirstDateWYR

Fun Fact
"Underwater basket weaving" became slang for easy college courses in the 1950s.

Would you Rather...

Begin by attempting a synchronized pogo-ball routine,

or

a "sword-fighting" lesson using giant inflatable flamingos?

Reflection
Graceful romance or ER visit waiting to happen.

Share It
Which prop fight makes you go viral for all the wrong reasons? #FirstDateWYR

Fun Fact
Inflatable pool toys were first mass-produced in the 1940s.

The Date Activity Nobody Asked For

Would you Rather...

Do your first date at a silent disco inside a laundromat,

or

at a unicycle riding class in a parking garage?

Reflection
Nothing says "true love" like sweat and concrete.

Share It
Which absurd venue would kill the mood faster — spin cycle or tire squeal?
#FirstDateWYR

Fun Fact
Silent discos began in the early 2000s as a way to avoid noise curfews.

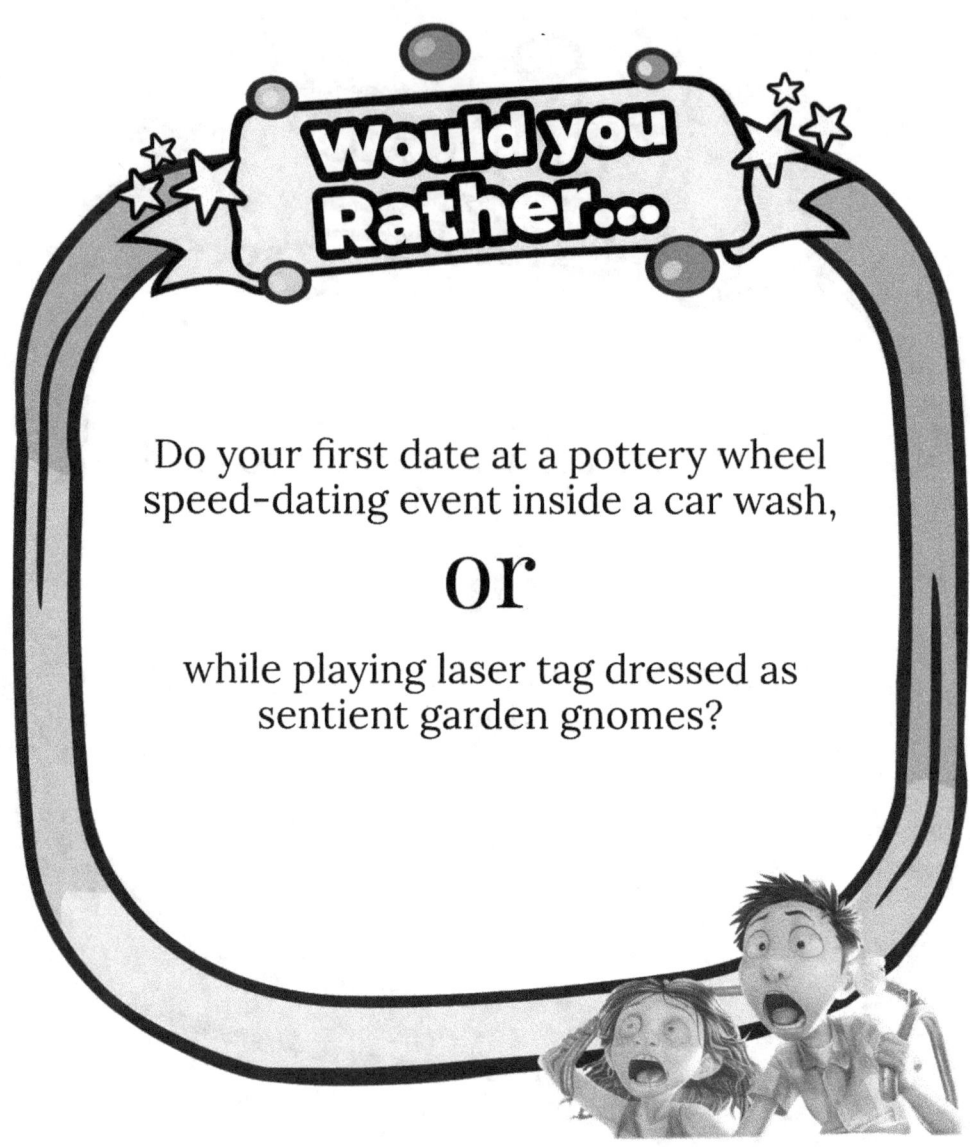

Do your first date at a pottery wheel speed-dating event inside a car wash,

or

while playing laser tag dressed as sentient garden gnomes?

Reflection
Nothing says romance like getting hose-blasted mid-ghosting or ducking behind a toadstool with a foam beard.

Share It
Which one gets you a second date faster — a full rinse cycle or a sneak attack with a plastic mushroom? #FirstDateWYR

Fun Fact
Laser tag was invented in 1979 and originally designed for military combat training before becoming a chaotic date-night staple.

Would you Rather...

Compete in a hot-air balloon jousting match,

or

attempt mechanical bull painting portraits of each other mid-ride?

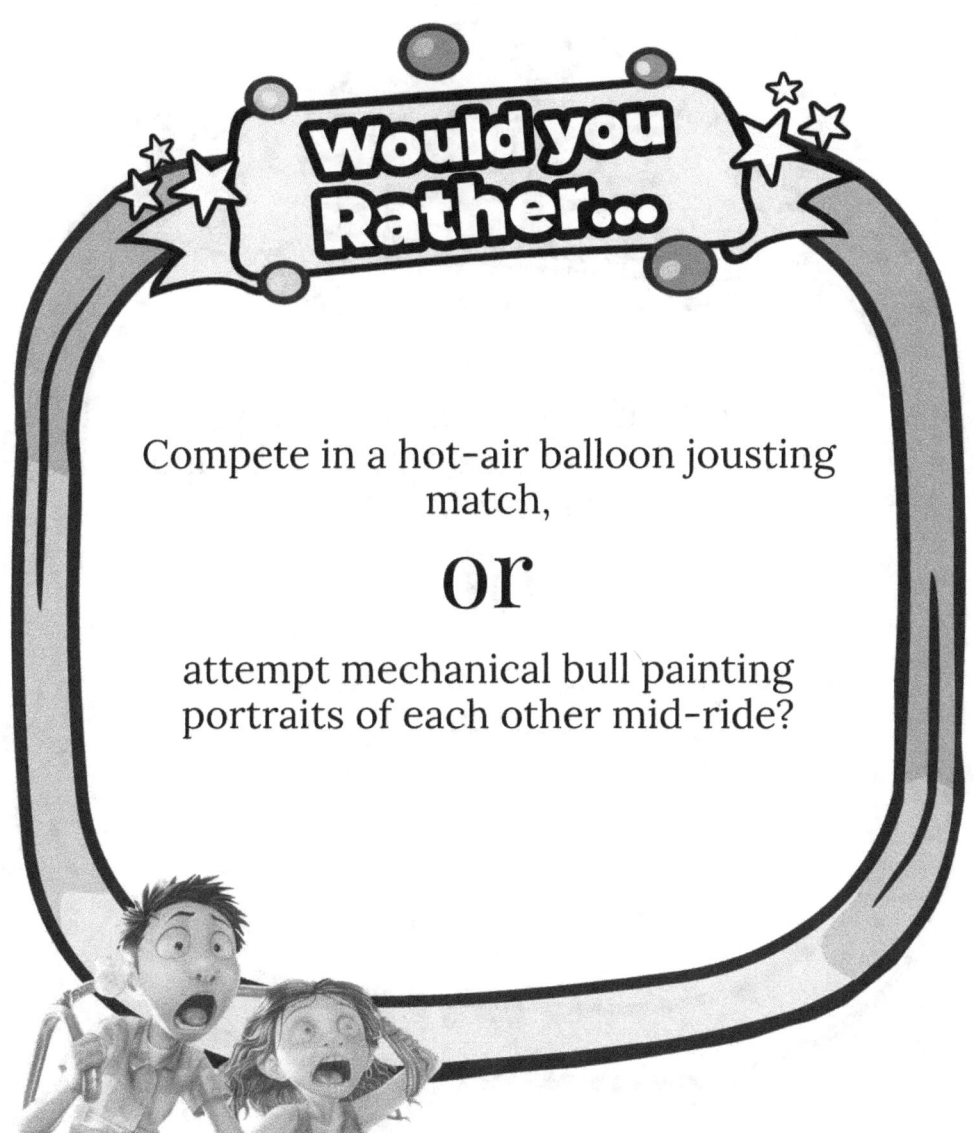

Reflection
Both are art projects in the language of concussions.

Share It
Which activity gets you a TikTok fan club faster? #FirstDateWYR

Fun Fact
The first hot-air balloon flight took place in Paris in 1783.

Would you Rather...

Start things off by auditioning as background zombies for a low-budget horror film,

or

entering a "fastest scream" contest at the park?

Reflection
Romance? No. Trauma bonding? Absolutely.

Share It
Which audition would shred your dignity (and vocal cords) faster? #FirstDateWYR

Fun Fact
The loudest human scream ever recorded reached 129 decibels.

Would you Rather...

Try to set a record for most marshmallows stuffed in your mouth,

or

for most hula hoops spun in a subway station?

Reflection
Either way, dignity melts before dessert.

Share It
Which humiliation reel would you send to your ex just to flex? #FirstDateWYR

Fun Fact
The 1958 hula hoop craze sold over 100 million hoops in six months.

Would you Rather...

Kick off the date by playing human curling on an ice rink (you're the stone),

or

bungee-jumping off a bridge while sipping milkshakes?

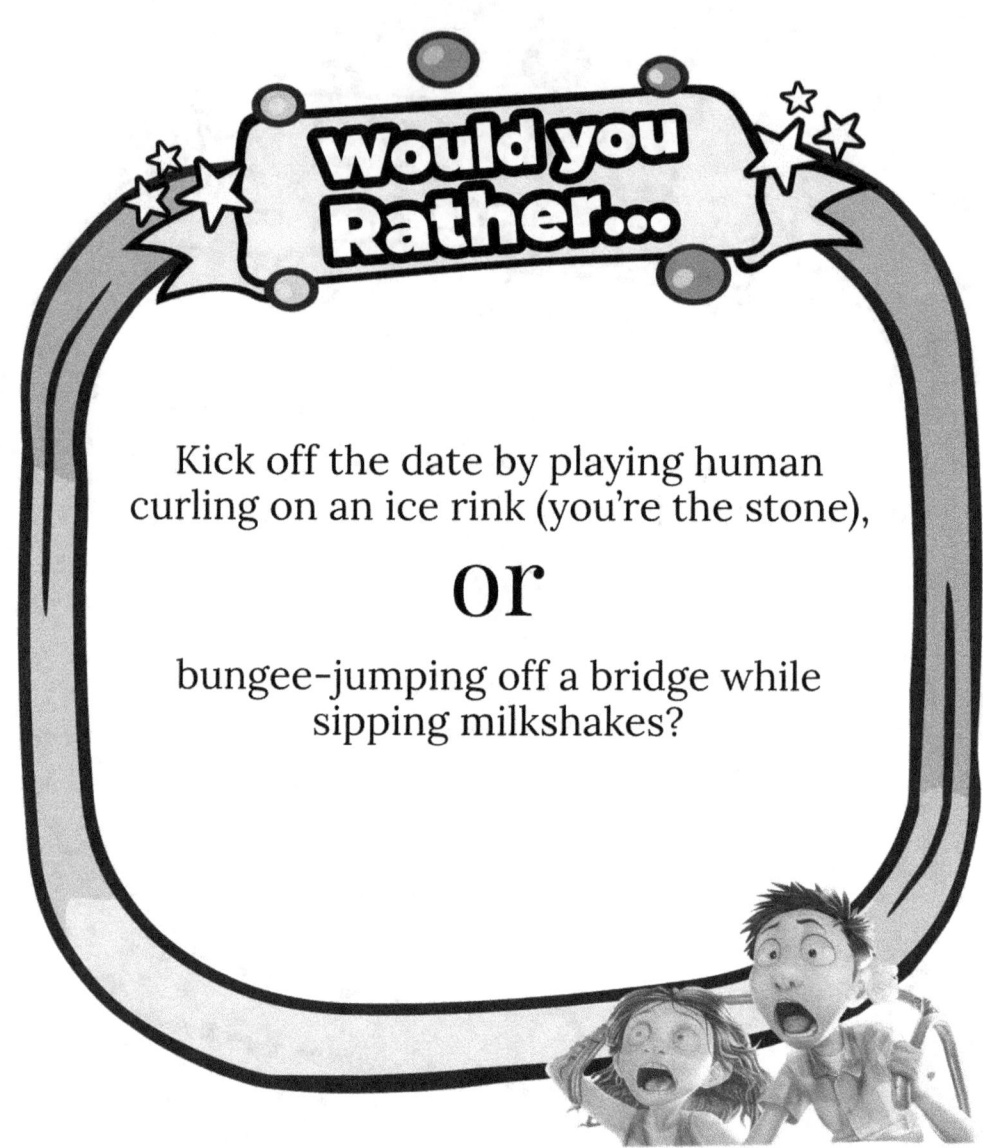

Reflection
Risking spine or stomach — love's a gamble.

Share It
Which extreme stunt gets you dumped before the second jump? #FirstDateWYR

Fun Fact
Curling stones are made of rare granite found in only two quarries worldwide.

Chapter 5 – Competitive Chaos

Vibe: The innocent fun turns into deranged competitions with ridiculous stakes and escalating absurdity.

Nothing says romance like sweating, shouting, and wildly inappropriate wagers.

Would you Rather...

Compete in a "who can ride the escalator longest without stepping off" showdown,

or

a "who can stare down a mall mannequin until security intervenes" contest?

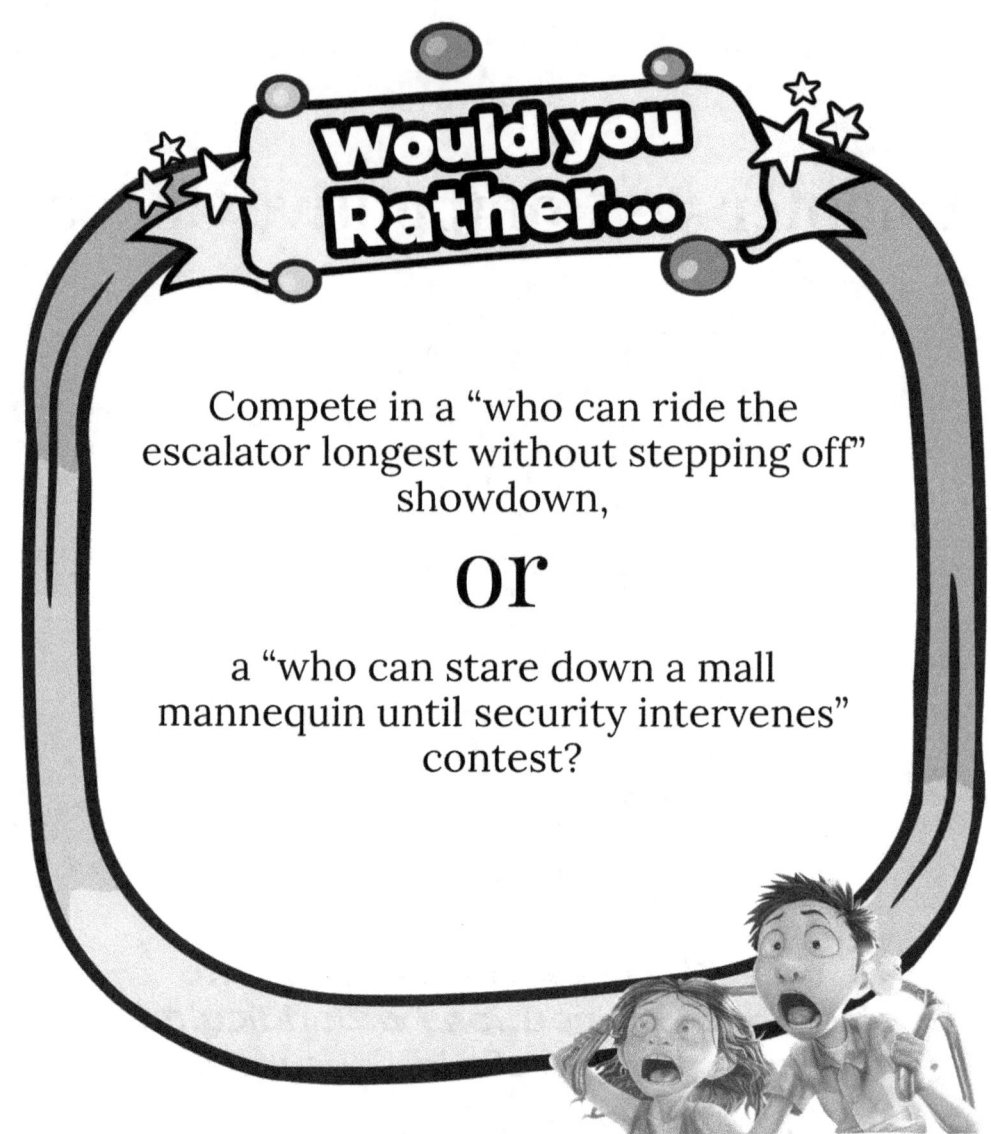

Reflection
That's not sport, that's mall loitering with extra steps.

Share It
Who's calling security first — the mall cop or your date? #FirstDateWYR

Fun Fact
The world's longest escalator is 450 feet in St. Petersburg, Russia.

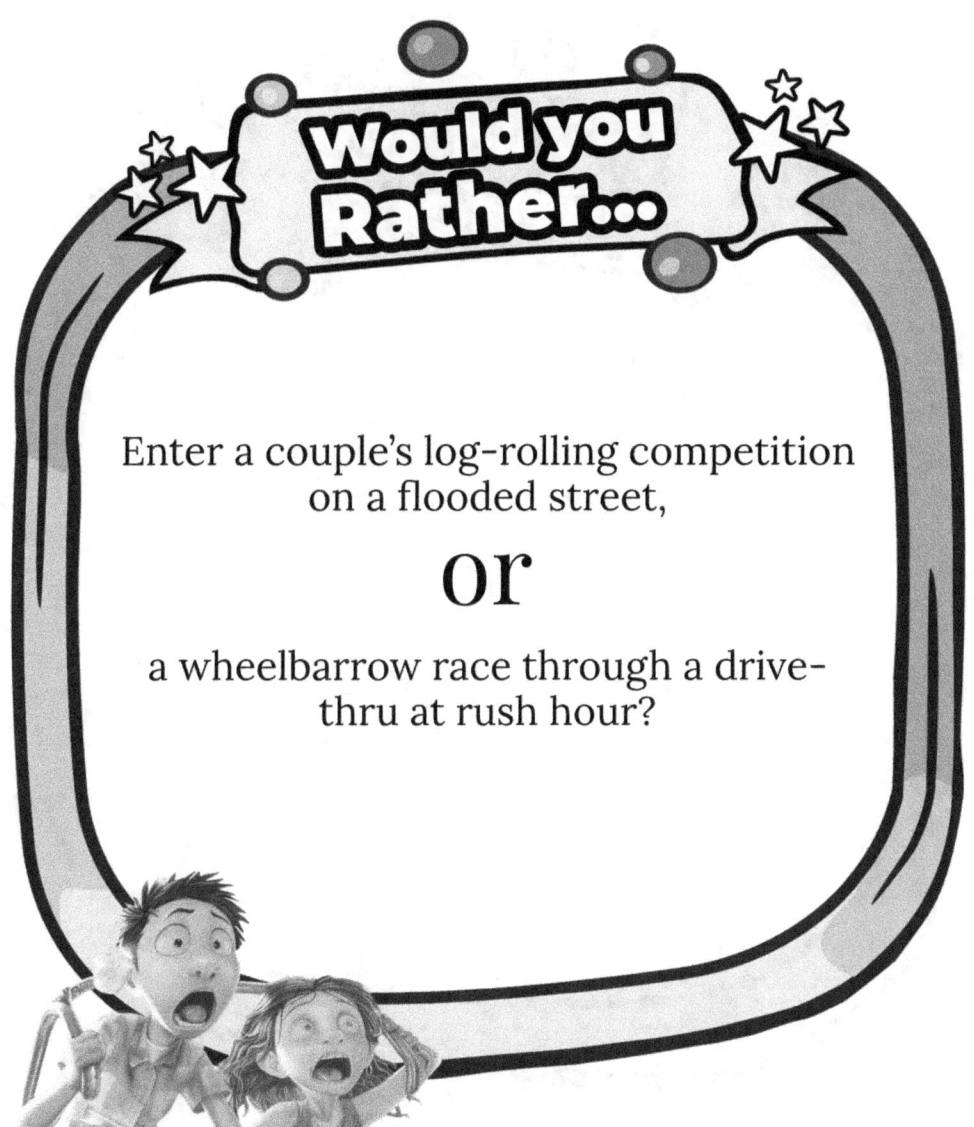

Would you Rather...

Enter a couple's log-rolling competition on a flooded street,

or

a wheelbarrow race through a drive-thru at rush hour?

Reflection
Win or lose, someone's fries are airborne.

Share It
Which viral video gets more views — soggy lumberjack love or McWheelbarrow mayhem? #FirstDateWYR

Fun Fact
Log rolling was popularized by lumberjacks in the 19th century.

Competitive Chaos

Would you Rather...

Compete in "extreme hula hoop battles" at a retirement home,

or

a belching contest inside a yoga studio?

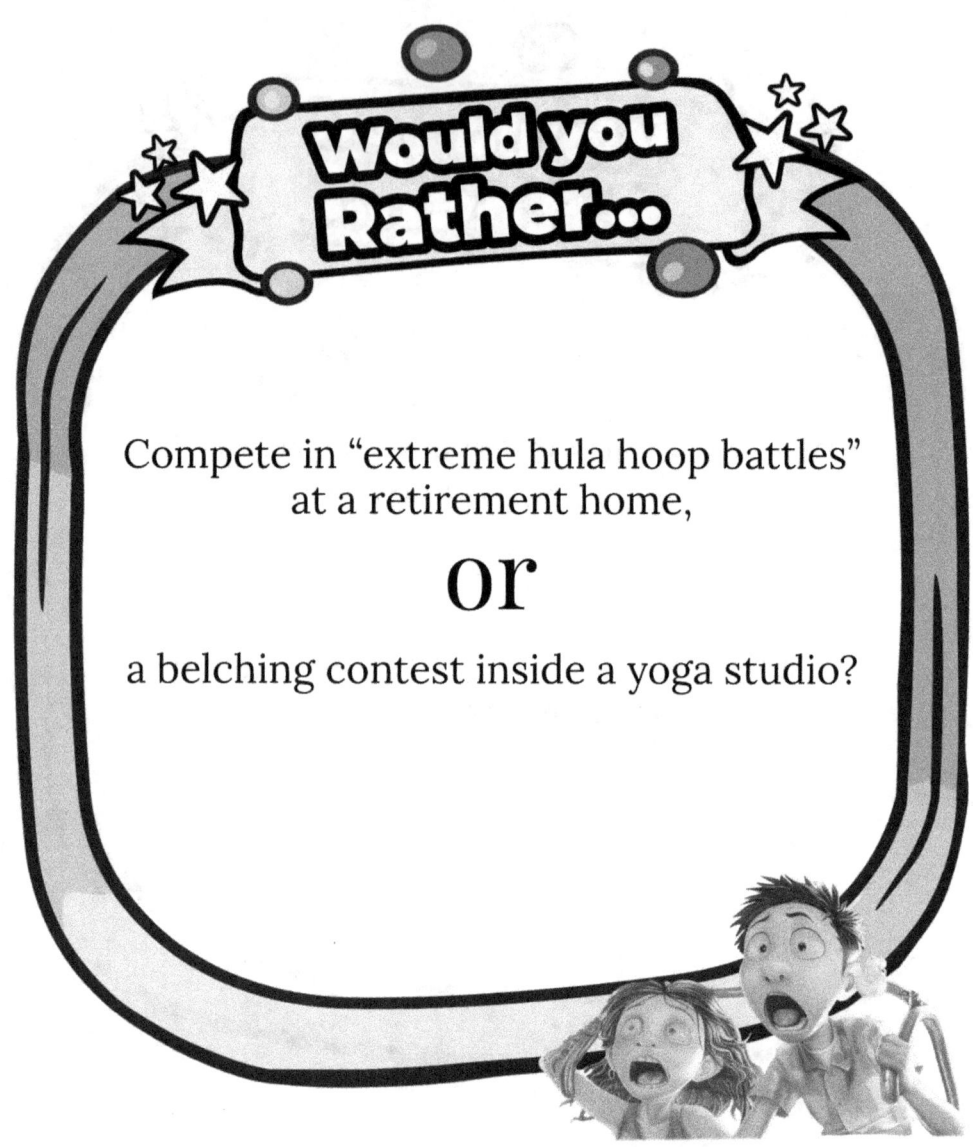

Reflection
Compete in "extreme hula hoop battles" at a retirement home, or a belching contest inside a yoga studio?

Share It
Compete in "extreme hula hoop battles" at a retirement home, or a belching contest inside a yoga studio?

Fun Fact
Compete in "extreme hula hoop battles" at a retirement home, or a belching contest inside a yoga studio?

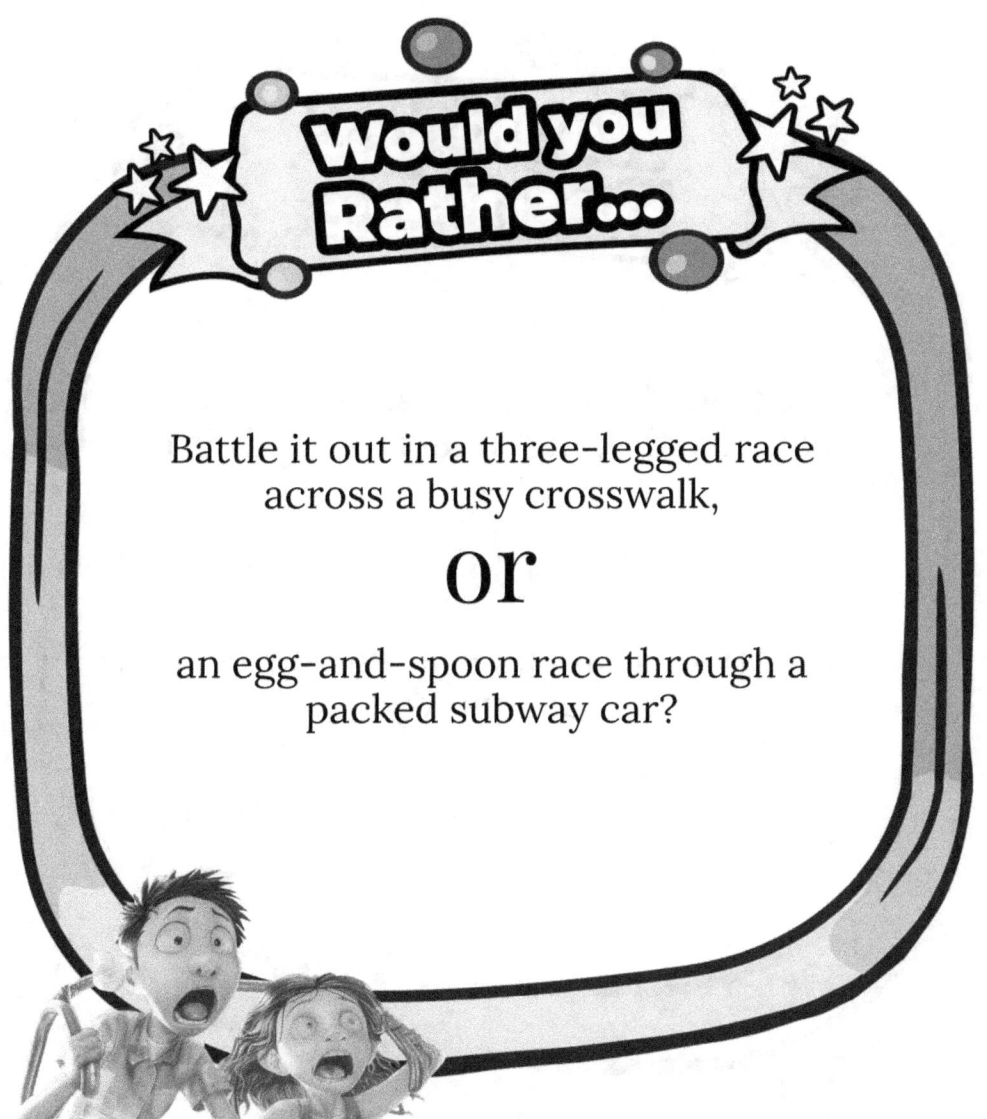

Would you Rather...

Battle it out in a three-legged race across a busy crosswalk,

or

an egg-and-spoon race through a packed subway car?

Reflection
Either way, you're ruining public transit for everyone.

Share It
Which commute disaster gets you trending under #DatingCrimes? #FirstDateWYR

Fun Fact
The three-legged race first appeared at 19th-century UK school fairs.

Would you Rather...

Go head-to-head in an "extreme pancake flipping" duel in a hardware store,

or

a whipped cream pie-eating contest at a dog park?

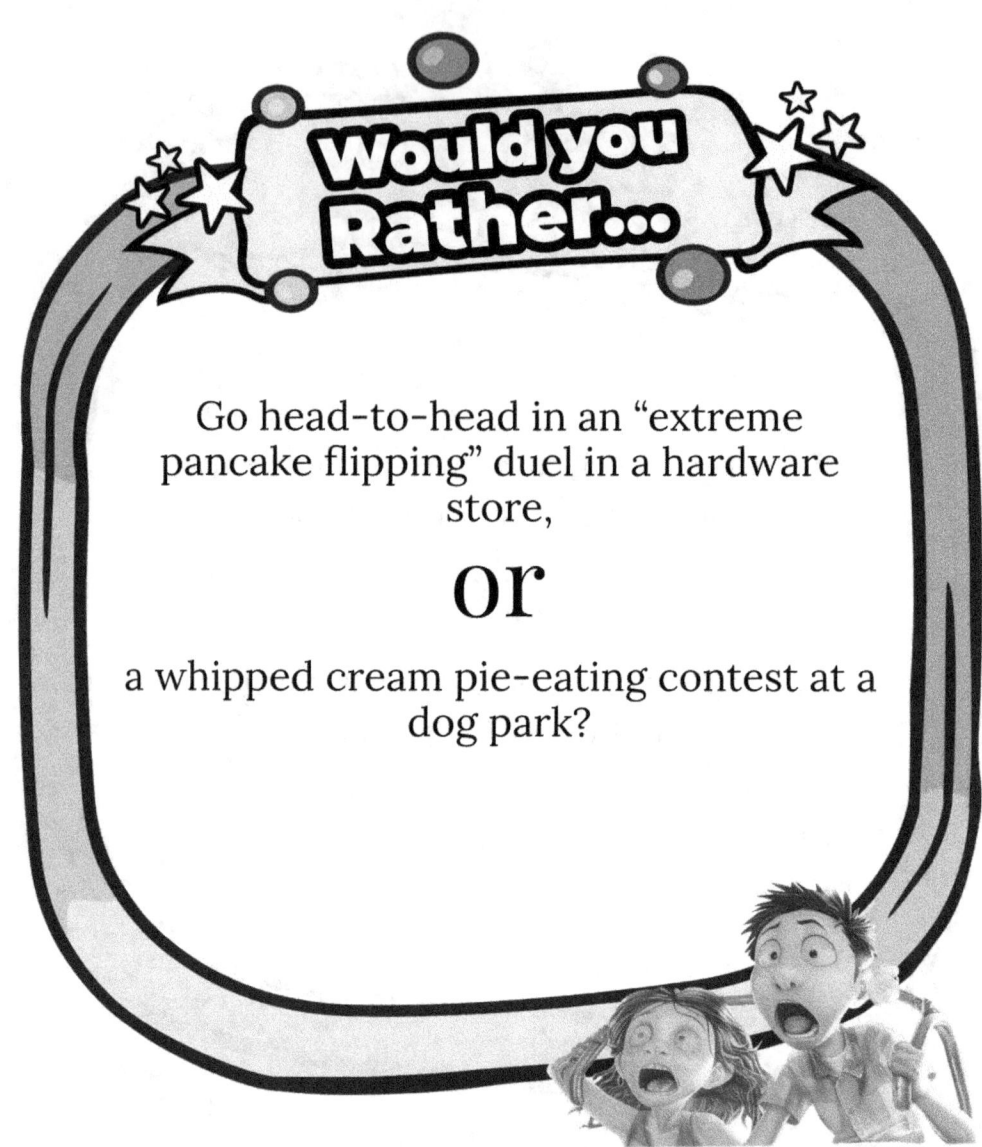

Reflection
Both sound like Yelp reviews nobody trusts.

Share It
Who's judging harder — the cashiers or the Chihuahuas? #FirstDateWYR

Fun Fact
The largest pancake ever cooked weighed over 6,600 pounds.

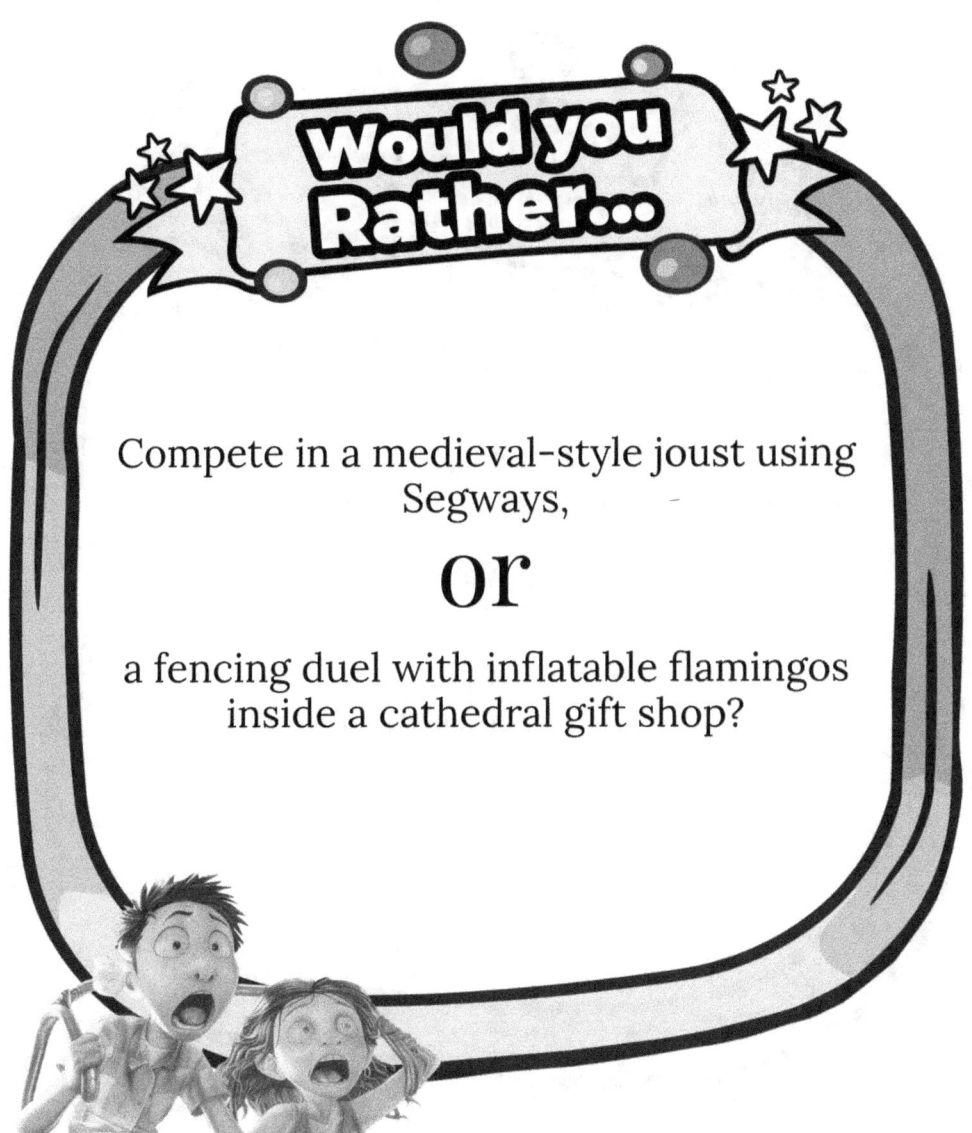

Would you Rather...

Compete in a medieval-style joust using Segways,

or

a fencing duel with inflatable flamingos inside a cathedral gift shop?

Reflection
Nothing screams romance like mall security chasing knights on wheels.

Share It
Which battle gets you banned from holy grounds first? #FirstDateWYR

Fun Fact
Segways were launched in 2001 but banned in several major cities within five years.

Would you Rather...

Enter a "fastest snow angel" contest in the frozen food aisle,

or

a synchronized shopping cart ballet in a Walmart parking lot?

Reflection
Forget romance — this is Olympic-level chaos.

Share It
Who's handing out medals — store security or TikTok? #FirstDateWYR

Fun Fact
Walmart parking lots are among the most common filming spots for viral dance videos.

Would you Rather...

Compete in a live "mattress surfing" race down a hotel staircase,

or

a blindfolded dodgeball match inside a crowded museum?

Reflection
Either way, someone's deductible is toast.

Share It
Which lawsuit would you rather explain to your insurance adjuster?
#FirstDateWYR

Fun Fact
Mattress surfing is banned in most dorms due to frequent injuries.

Competitive Chaos

Would you Rather...

Battle in a karaoke showdown using only opera screams,

or

a freestyle rap contest about tractor maintenance?

Reflection
You're not winning love, you're winning infamy.

Share It
Which clip would you send to your ex just to haunt them? #FirstDateWYR

Fun Fact
Rapper Twista once hit 11.2 syllables per second, a Guinness World Record.

Would you Rather...

End the night with a tug-of-war over a giant inflatable pickle,

or

a speed-building contest for a life-sized Jenga tower made of watermelons?

Reflection
Romance is dead. Produce-based warfare lives forever.

Share It
Who's getting kicked out first — Team Pickle or Team Melon?
#FirstDateWYR

Fun Fact
The largest Jenga tower ever built reached 40 levels tall.

Competitive Chaos | 61

Chapter 6 – Oversharing, Overhearing, Over It

Vibe: The "getting to know you" stage spirals into awkward confessions, bizarre hypotheticals, and intrusive background weirdness.

Your date now knows way too much about you… and somehow not enough.

Would you Rather...

Admit your biggest regret is losing a thumb war to a toddler,

or

that you once got grounded for selling invisible pets to neighbors?

Reflection
Either way, you peaked before you could drive.

Share It
Which confession ruins your dignity faster — Tiny Thumb Titan or Ghost Dog Scam?
#FirstDateWYR

Fun Fact
In the 1970s, millions of "pet rocks" were sold as a real fad.

Oversharing, Overhearing, Over It

Would you Rather...

Confess you once spent a whole vacation faking a British accent,

or

that you got kicked out of a history tour for trying to reenact it with shadow puppets made from your feet?

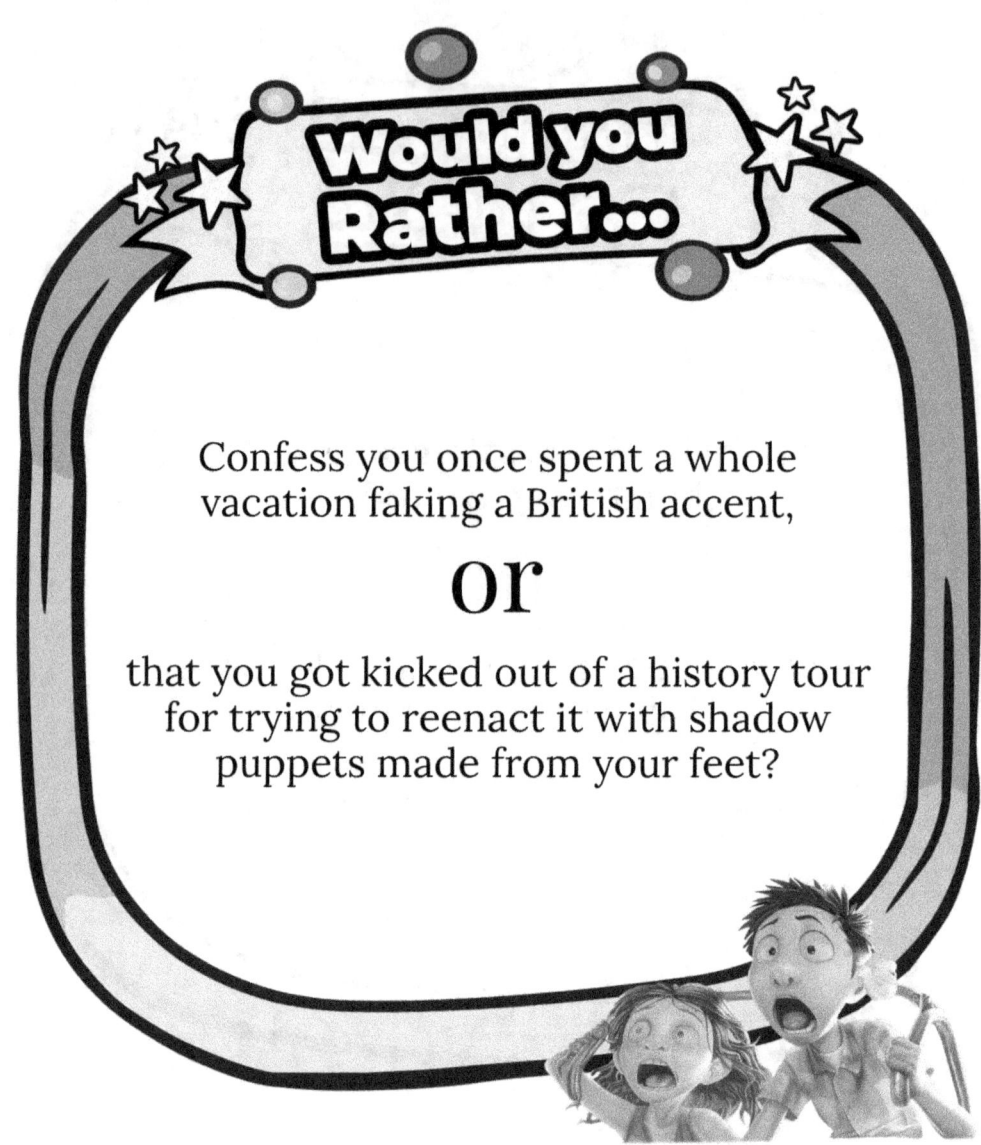

Reflection
One screams identity crisis, the other screams podiatry issues.

Share It
Which story would you admit without crying — Royal Faker or Toe Puppet Theatre? #FirstDateWYR

Fun Fact
Shadow puppetry has been practiced for over 2,000 years, with origins traced to China and India.

Would you Rather...

Reveal you cried when a carnival goldfish outlived your childhood dog,

or

that you hosted a funeral service for your dead houseplant?

Reflection
The emotional scale is... confusing.

Share It
Which memorial service deserves a Netflix special — "Goldie Forever" or "Fern's Final Farewell"?
#FirstDateWYR

Fun Fact
Some goldfish have lived more than 40 years in captivity.

Would you Rather...

Admit your personal mascot is a traffic cone because it "warns people,"

or

that you once listed "bubble wrap stomping" as a résumé skill?

Reflection
Neither screams "leadership potential."

Share It
Which confession gets you laughed out of an interview faster? #FirstDateWYR

Fun Fact
Bubble wrap was originally invented as wallpaper in 1957.

Would you Rather...

Tell your date you once broke up with someone because they sneezed like a trumpet,

or

because they refused to eat curly fries?

Reflection
Both are dealbreakers that deserve side-eye.

Share It
Which breakup would your group chat roast you for harder? #FirstDateWYR

Fun Fact
The longest recorded sneezing fit lasted 978 days.

Would you Rather...

Confess your favorite childhood toy was a parking meter,

or

that you once built a family tree for your sock collection?

Reflection
No one said hobbies had to be healthy.

Share It
Which one gets you reported to a therapist faster? #FirstDateWYR

Fun Fact
The first coin-operated parking meter was installed in Oklahoma City in 1935.

Would you Rather...

Reveal you once mailed RSVP invitations to your furniture,

or

that you tried to teach your reflection how to high-five?

Reflection
Social life: non-existent. Comedy: flawless.

Share It
Which ritual would you actually admit to a therapist — Chair Wedding or Mirror High-Five? #FirstDateWYR

Fun Fact
In many cultures, mirrors were once thought to contain fragments of the soul.

Would you Rather...

Admit you once ruined a birthday party by spoiling a magician's finale,

or

that you derailed a spelling bee by cheering for the dictionary?

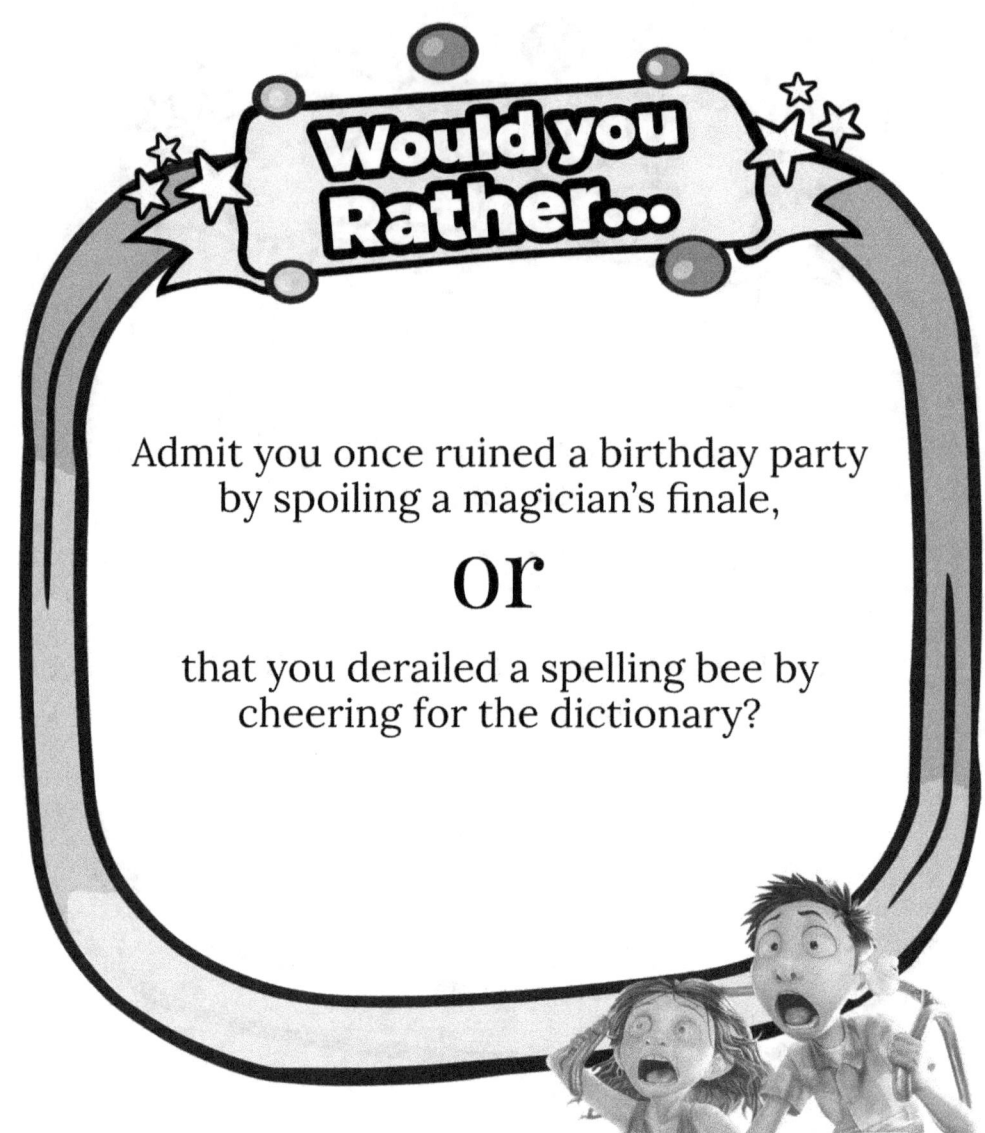

Reflection
Honestly, both are chaotic power moves.

Share It
Which sabotage would you brag about like it was a life achievement? #FirstDateWYR

Fun Fact
The first U.S. national spelling bee was held in 1925.

Would you Rather...

Share that you once rated your burps on a five-star scale,

or

that you kept a scrapbook of ATM error messages?

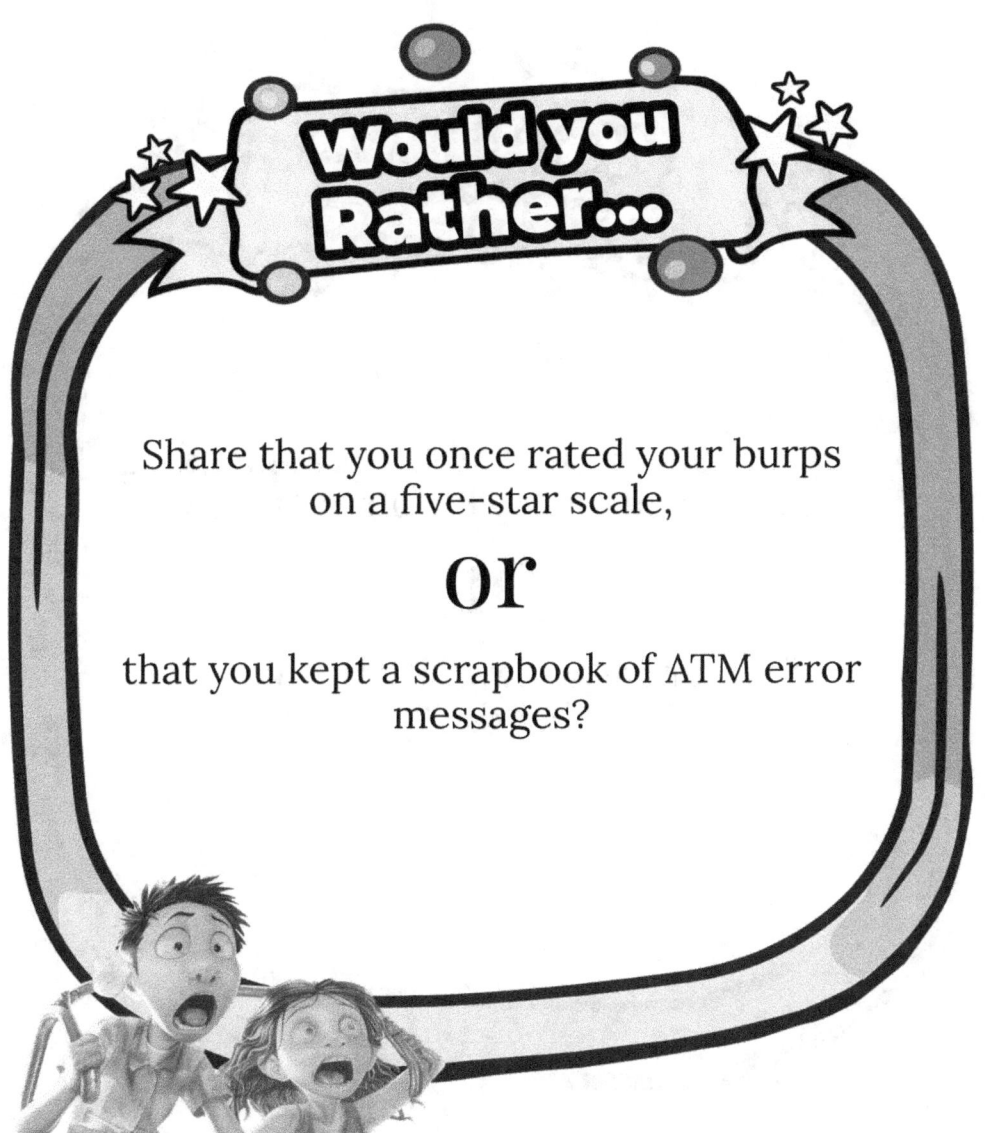

Reflection
At least you're documenting something... sort of.

Share It
Which collection would you admit to first — Burp Reviews or ATM Diaries? #FirstDateWYR

Fun Fact
The average burp releases about half a liter of gas from the stomach.

Would you Rather...

Reveal you got in trouble for applauding at the end of a CPR training video,

or

for starting a slow clap at a court hearing?

Reflection
Romance ends where awkward clapping begins.

Share It
Which clap fail would haunt you longer — Medical Encore or Courtroom Ovation? #FirstDateWYR

Fun Fact
The "slow clap" trope first appeared in movies in the 1980s.

Chapter 7 – Snack Break from Hell

Vibe: The "casual bite" portion of the date becomes a culinary catastrophe, featuring foods, drinks, and settings no human should endure.

You're not just losing your appetite — you're questioning your will to live.

Would you Rather...

Sip from a cocktail served in a lightbulb that delivers tiny electric shocks with each sip,

or

share a slushie made entirely of blended turnips?

Reflection
One's a science experiment, the other's a farmer's revenge.

Share It
Which sip destroys your dignity faster — Shocktail or Root Slush? #FirstDateWYR

Fun Fact
Early novelty glassware designs included actual lab equipment, but drinking from a powered bulb is a new level of reckless.

Would you Rather...

Try to eat spaghetti using only a hair straightener,

or

sip soup through a mildly chewed bendy straw on national television?

Reflection
One turns your lunch into a hair tutorial, the other into a health code violation in HD.

Share It
Which would ruin your reputation faster — steam-pressed pasta or public slurpage? #FirstDateWYR

Fun Fact
The modern bendy straw was invented in 1937 by a man who saw his daughter struggling to drink from a straight straw.

Would you Rather...

Eat soup inside a sombrero while someone else is wearing it and dancing the jig,

or

popcorn drenched in glow-in-the-dark "mystery butter"?

Reflection
Dinner and a show, but no encore.

Share It
Which dish would you risk food poisoning for first? #FirstDateWYR

Fun Fact
Sombreros were designed for shade but have been repurposed in modern novelty dining stunts.

Snack Break from Hell

Would you Rather...

Accidentally order "pond scum punch" with floating algae,

or

sip a smoothie thickened with industrial-strength glue?

Reflection
Hydration just became sabotage.

Share It
Which glass would you politely gag into? #FirstDateWYR

Fun Fact
Cyanobacteria (pond scum) helped oxygenate Earth billions of years ago.

Would you Rather...

Bite into a churro stuffed with marbles,

or

a donut that squirts cold spaghetti?

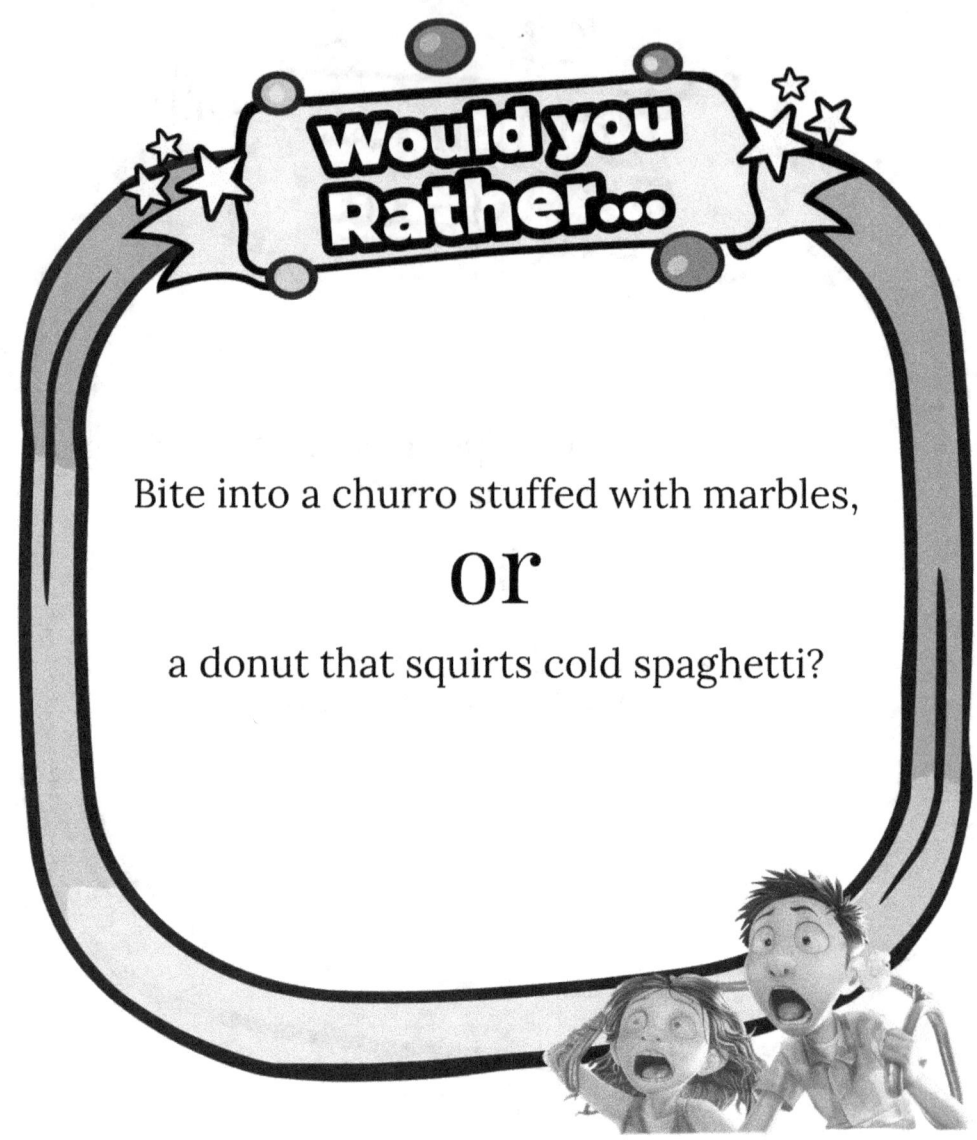

Reflection
Dessert roulette is never a safe game.

Share It
Which filling ends your appetite faster? #FirstDateWYR

Fun Fact
The first automated donut machine was patented in 1920.

Would you Rather...

Have your date hand-feed you a giant fortune cookie so big you could crawl inside,

or

a fruit roll-up so long it has its own postal code?

Reflection
Romance or real estate investment?

Share It
Which snack nightmare would you post on Zillow? #FirstDateWYR

Fun Fact
The world's largest fortune cookie weighed over 1,300 pounds.

Snack Break from Hell | 79

Would you Rather...

Watch your soda cup melt in your hand like wax,

or

discover your iced tea is actually dirty dishwater "infused with authenticity"?

Reflection
Suddenly bottled water feels luxurious.

Share It
Which beverage lie would you sip just to look polite?
#FirstDateWYR

Fun Fact
Tannins in wetlands often make water look like brewed tea.

80 | Snack Break from Hell

Would you Rather...

Accidentally snack on nacho-flavored drywall chips,

or

cheese puffs that squeak like mice when bitten?

Reflection
Either way, silence isn't happening.

Share It
Which crunch gets you ghosted mid-snack? #FirstDateWYR

Fun Fact
Edible packaging made from milk proteins is in active development today.

Would you Rather...

End up with pudding that expands like quicksand,

or

ice cream that hardens into concrete mid-bite?

Reflection
Dessert shouldn't require emergency services.

Share It
Which failed dessert would you still try for clout? #FirstDateWYR

Fun Fact
The concept of instant pudding dates back to 1918 by My-T-Fine.

Would you Rather...

Accidentally sip coffee with a live goldfish swimming in it,

or

tea poured out of an old boot at a historical reenactment brunch?

Reflection
Both are liquid regret with garnish.

Share It
Which beverage disaster would you never admit to anyone — goldfish macchiato or sole-infused steep? #FirstDateWYR

Fun Fact
In WWII, soldiers sometimes brewed tea in boots when teapots were scarce.

Snack Break from Hell

Chapter 8 – The Universe Interrupts

Vibe: Random chaos and intrusions derail any chance of normalcy. The world itself seems to want this date to fail.

It's less "romantic outing," more "biblical plague in skinny jeans."

Would you Rather...

Be trapped together on an out-of-service ski lift in July,

or

lost inside a hedge maze that suddenly locks from the outside?

Reflection
Love finds a way... or it doesn't.

Share It
Which nightmare screams "soulmate test" harder — Suspended Summer or Maze Prison? #FirstDateWYR

Fun Fact
The world's largest hedge maze is in Hawaii, covering three acres.

The Universe Interrupts

Would you Rather...

Accidentally join a competitive porcupine grooming contest,

or

get registered as surprise entrants in a dog obedience show?

Reflection
Either way, somebody's bleeding or barking.

Share It
Which pet pageant exposes your flaws faster — Spiky Spa or Dog Drill Team? #FirstDateWYR

Fun Fact
Porcupines have up to 30,000 quills that detach easily when touched.

Would you Rather...

Your date gets mistaken for the keynote speaker at a dental convention,

or

for the auctioneer at a livestock sale?

Reflection
The confidence test of a lifetime.

Share It
Which stage disaster would you fake your way through — Teeth Talk or Cow Sale? #FirstDateWYR

Fun Fact
The world record for fastest auctioneer speech exceeds 400 words per minute.

Would you Rather...

Get suddenly swept into a Zorbing race down a hill,

or

a spontaneous human chess match in the middle of a city square?

Reflection
Love is a battlefield... literally.

Share It
Which bizarre sport makes you surrender first? #FirstDateWYR

Fun Fact
Zorbing originated in New Zealand in the 1990s.

Would you Rather...

The entire floor beneath you slowly tilts like a funhouse,

or

the walls start closing in just enough to make you shuffle closer together?

Reflection
Romance by architectural malfunction.

Share It
Which panic-inducing setting feels more like fate — Tilted Love or Creeping Walls? #FirstDateWYR

Fun Fact
"Funhouse" architecture dates back to 19th-century European fairs.

Would you Rather...

A stranger hands you a live turkey vulture and vanishes,

or

someone straps a sandwich board to your chest advertising "World's Saddest Date"?

Reflection
Neither comes with instructions.

Share It
Which disaster would you actually try to style out? #FirstDateWYR

Fun Fact
Turkey vultures can detect carrion from over a mile away with their sense of smell.

Would you Rather...

Your date keeps getting interrupted by people begging for autographs as the star of an adult diaper commercial,

or

by neighbors returning dozens of stolen garden gnomes to your table?

Reflection
Fame is fleeting, gnomes are forever.

Share It
Which false identity would you roll with longer — Diaper Icon or Gnome King? #FirstDateWYR

Fun Fact
The first mass-produced garden gnomes were made in Germany in the 1800s.

Would you Rather...

The lights suddenly black out and you're spotlighted on a rotating stage,

or

you're both dragged onto a float in a Santa Claus parade... in April?

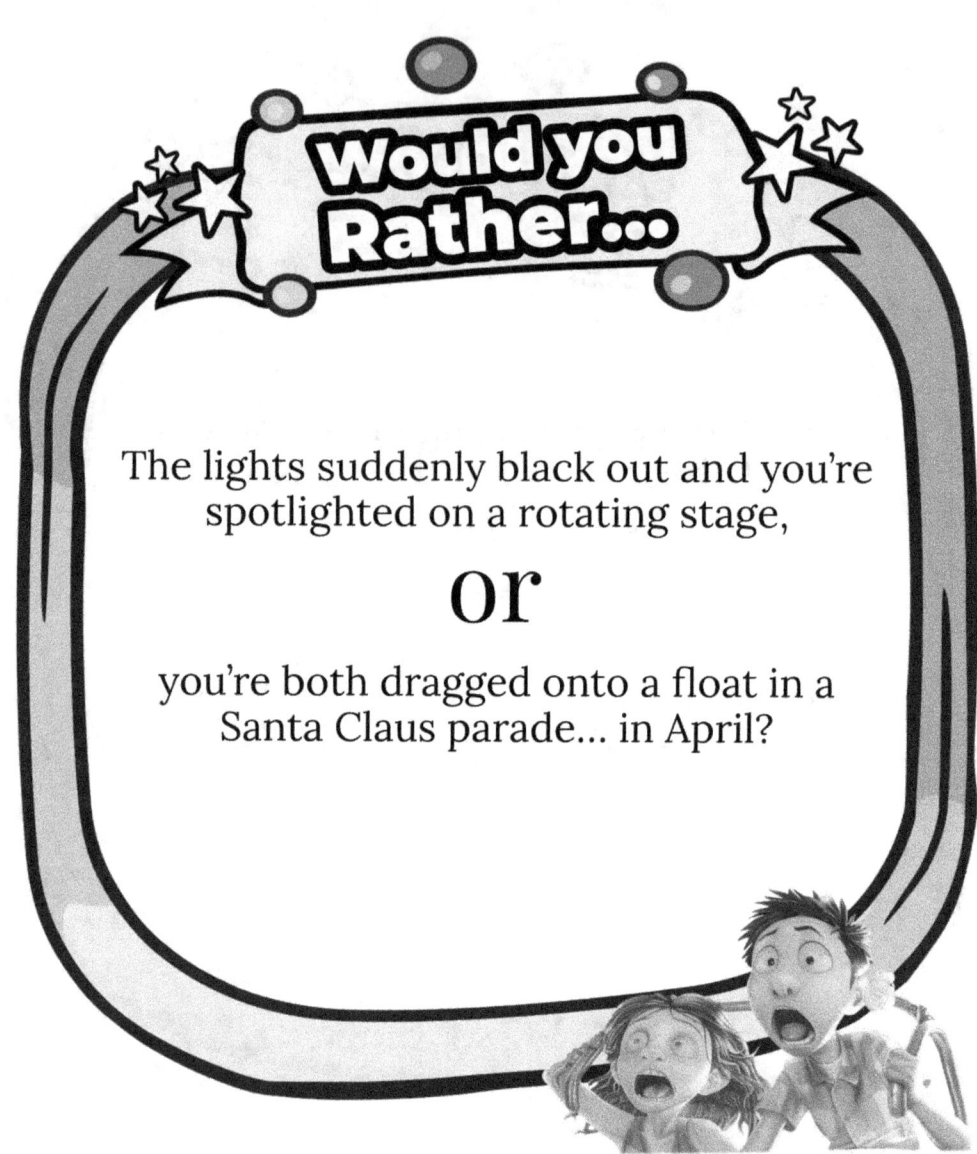

Reflection
Nothing like seasonal confusion.

Share It
Which humiliation is harder to explain — Stage Prison or April Claus? #FirstDateWYR

Fun Fact
The world's largest Santa Claus parade takes place in Toronto every November.

Would you Rather...

Try to maintain eye contact while 200 Roombas burst out of a sinkhole mid-date,

or

casually keep eating as frogs rain exclusively on your table?

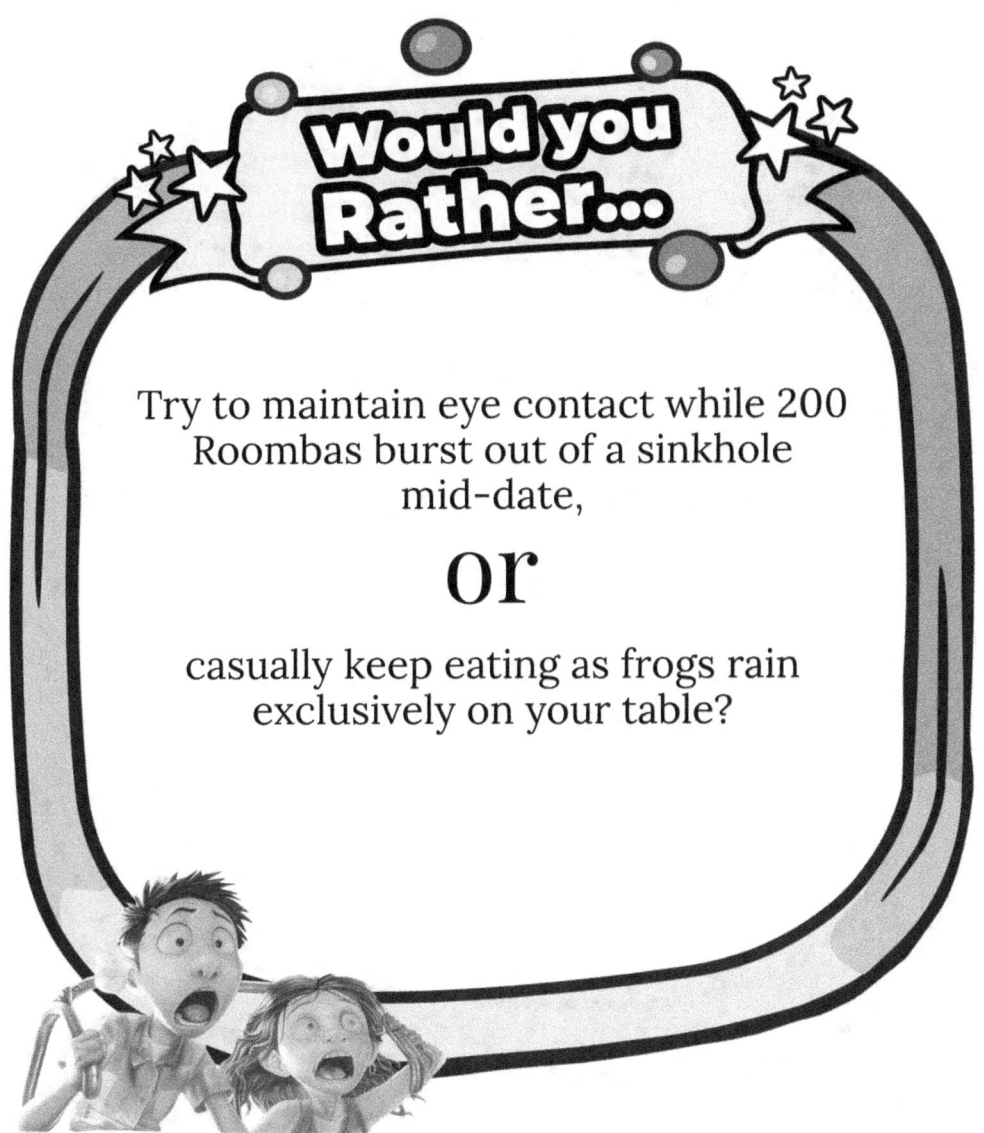

Reflection
Romance really tests your poker face when amphibians are flopping into your soup or robot vacuums are forming a conga line.

Share It
Which moment would you pretend was totally normal — Roomba rave or frog fondue? #FirstDateWYR

Fun Fact
Roombas have been used in experimental art performances, including dance choreography, painting, and an opera, replacing backup dancers.

Would you Rather...

A giant animatronic dinosaur malfunctions and follows you around,

or

a kangaroo boxing match suddenly erupts around your table?

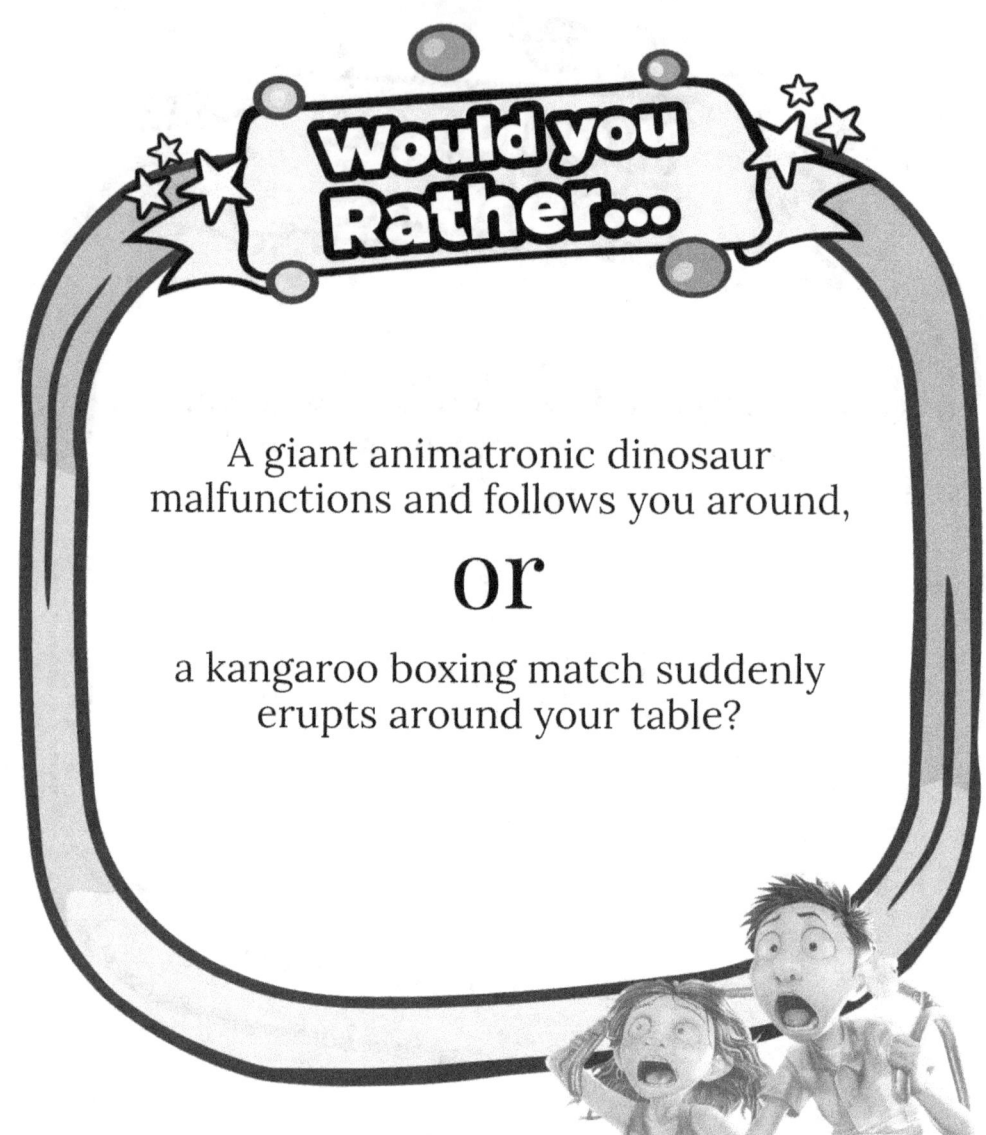

Reflection
Prehistoric awkwardness or marsupial mayhem.

Share It
Which public nightmare would you actually outlast? #FirstDateWYR

Fun Fact
Kangaroo boxing exhibitions were once a controversial circus act.

Chapter 9 – The Desperate Recovery Attempt

Vibe: Awkward efforts to steer things back to "normal" only make things way, way worse.

Like putting glitter on a dumpster fire — shiny, but still burning.

Would you Rather...

Sit calmly while a sprinkler blasts sticky, melted candy,

or

while a wind machine pelts you both with confetti for twenty minutes straight?

Reflection
Nothing says "romance" like being coated in syrup or parade debris.

Share It
Which mess would you fake a smile through? #FirstDateWYR

Fun Fact
The largest confetti cannon ever fired launched over 1,000 pounds of confetti in Italy.

Would you Rather...

Pretend everything's fine while holding hands inside a giant foam mascot suit,

or

while both of you are accidentally zip-tied together by a rogue security guard?

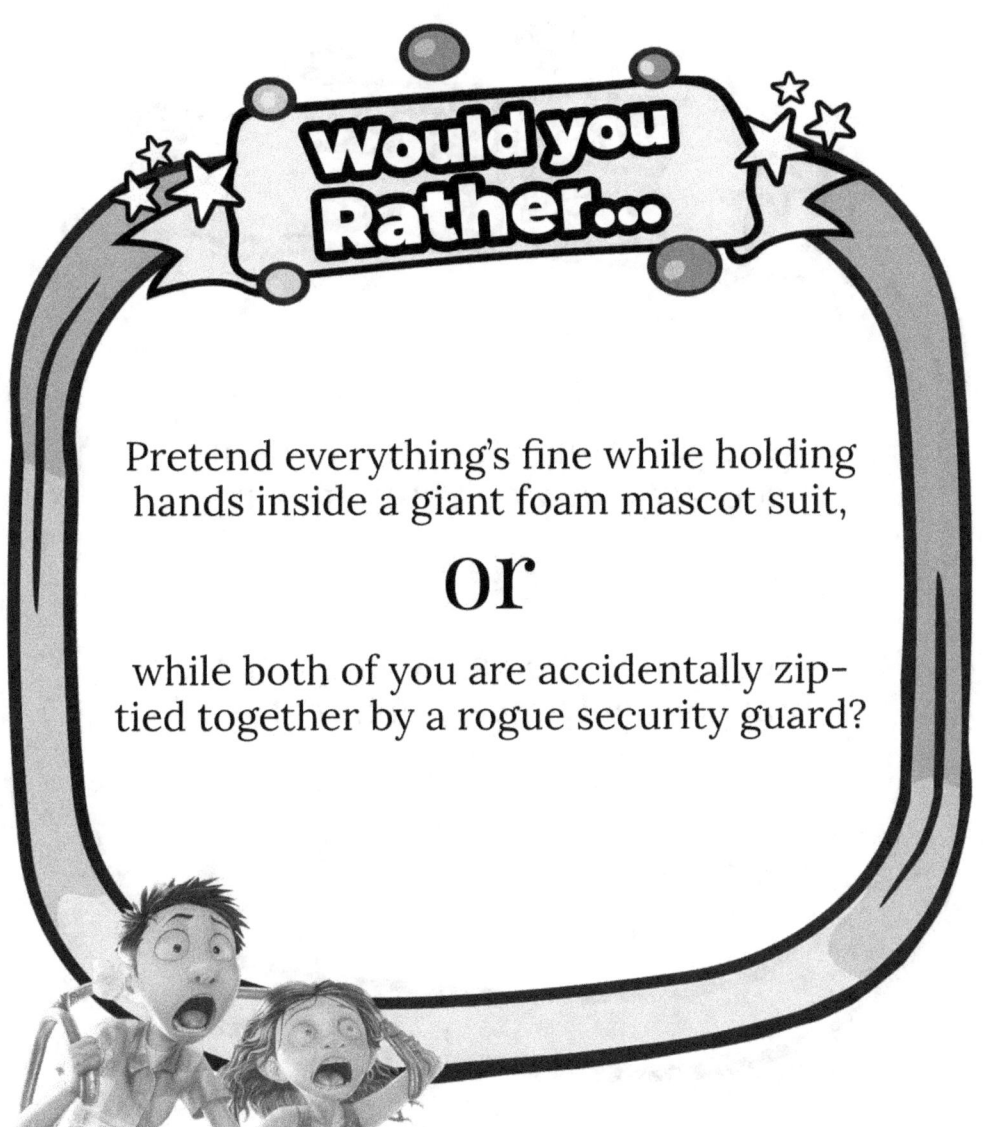

Reflection
Nothing ruins small talk faster than "do you have scissors?"

Share It
Which would end the date faster? #FirstDateWYR

Fun Fact
The Guinness World Record for largest mascot gathering was 134 in Japan, 2013.

The Desperate Recovery Attempt

Would you Rather...

Keep chatting while perched on a seesaw that won't stop moving,

or

while standing on a moving walkway that suddenly reverses directions?

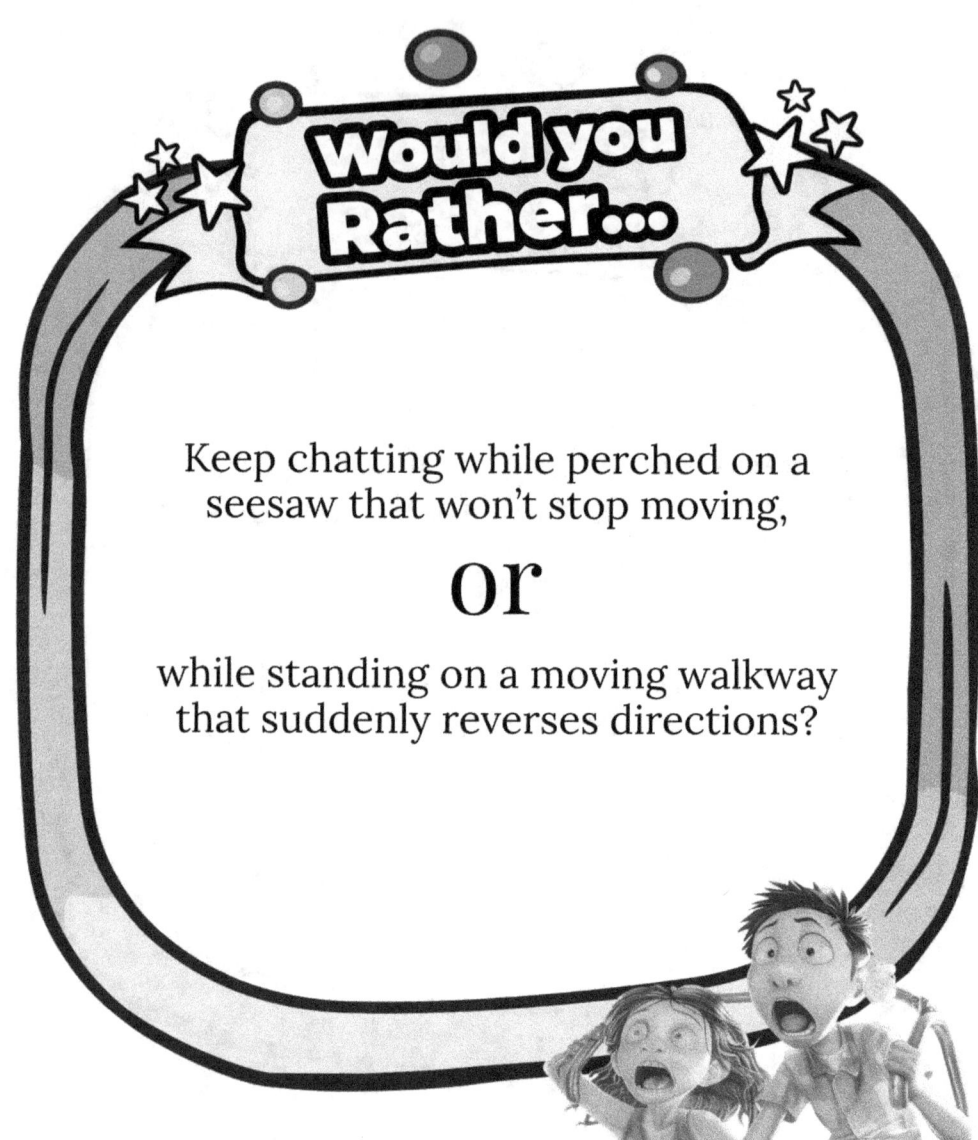

Reflection
Gravity is the world's worst wingman.

Share It
Which "just act natural" setting would betray you? #FirstDateWYR

Fun Fact
The first moving walkway was installed at the 1900 Paris Exposition.

Would you Rather...

Smile politely as you're carried away by a rogue parade float shaped like a giant toilet,

or

buried under popcorn that keeps shooting out of a t-shirt cannon?

Reflection
Either way, dignity gets cancelled.

Share It
Which disaster headline would you star in first? #FirstDateWYR

Fun Fact
The world's largest popcorn ball weighed over 9,000 pounds.

The Desperate Recovery Attempt

Would you Rather...

Pretend you're unfazed while both of you get trapped inside a malfunctioning photo booth that keeps spitting out mugshots of strangers,

or

while an animatronic fortune teller loudly announces your "doomed marriage" to the crowd?

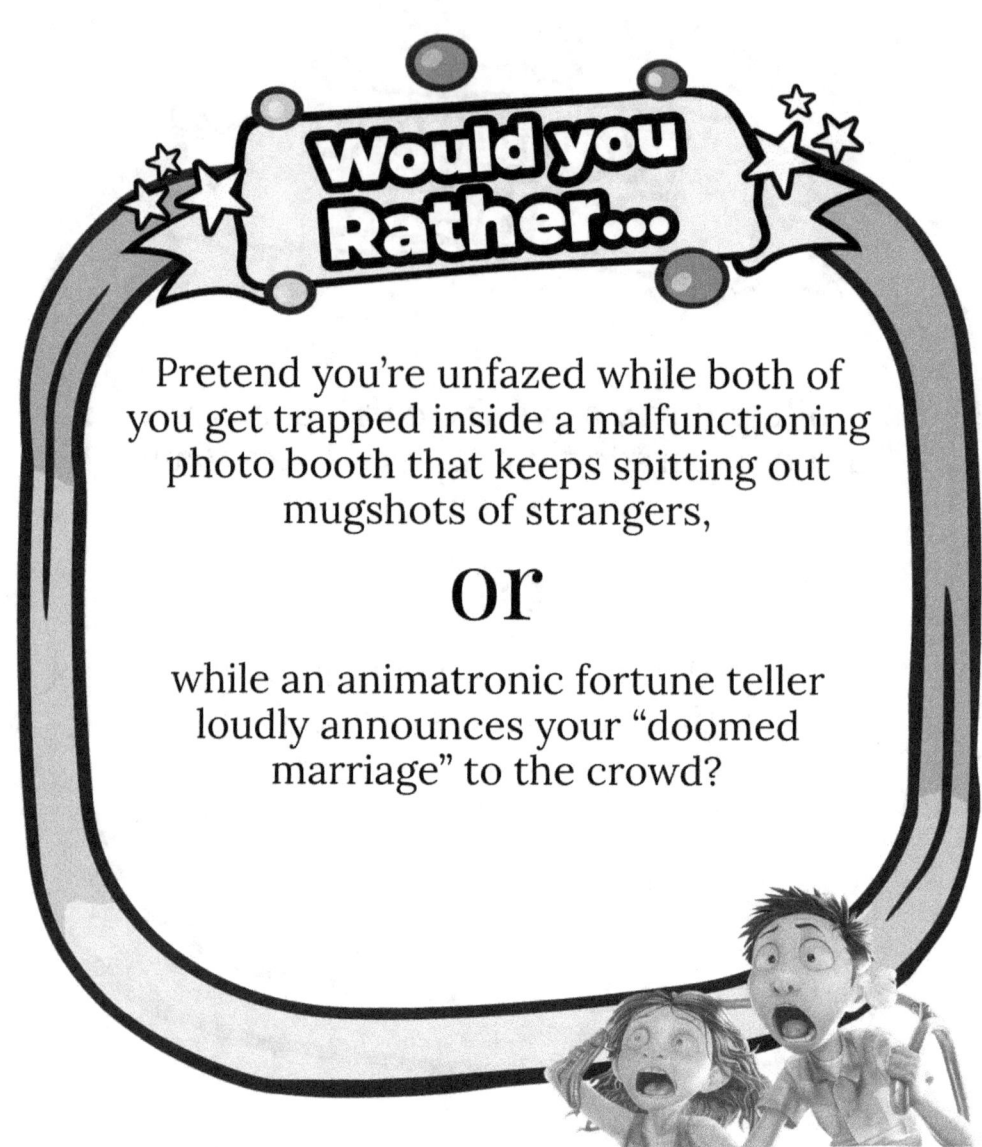

Reflection
Nothing kills small talk faster than a robot predicting divorce before appetizers.

Share It
Which mechanical meltdown would you fake a smile through? #FirstDateWYR

Fun Fact
The first animatronic fortune teller, "Grandmother's Predictions," debuted at the 1893 Chicago World's Fair.

Would you Rather...

Keep sipping your drink while your table slowly tips like a sinking ship,

or

while the entire floor starts vibrating like an uninvited dance battle?

Reflection
Romance thrives in controlled environments, not earthquake chic.

Share It
Which malfunction screams "we'll never recover"? #FirstDateWYR

Fun Fact
Tokyo's earthquake simulators can replicate quakes up to magnitude 7.

The Desperate Recovery Attempt

Would you Rather...

Try to maintain conversation as an improv troupe insists you're part of their performance,

or

as a group of tourists keeps mistaking you for a wax museum display?

Reflection
Flirting is hard enough without being heckled or posed.

Share It
Which disaster would you crack first? #FirstDateWYR

Fun Fact
Madame Tussauds in London opened in 1835 and now attracts 2.5 million visitors a year.

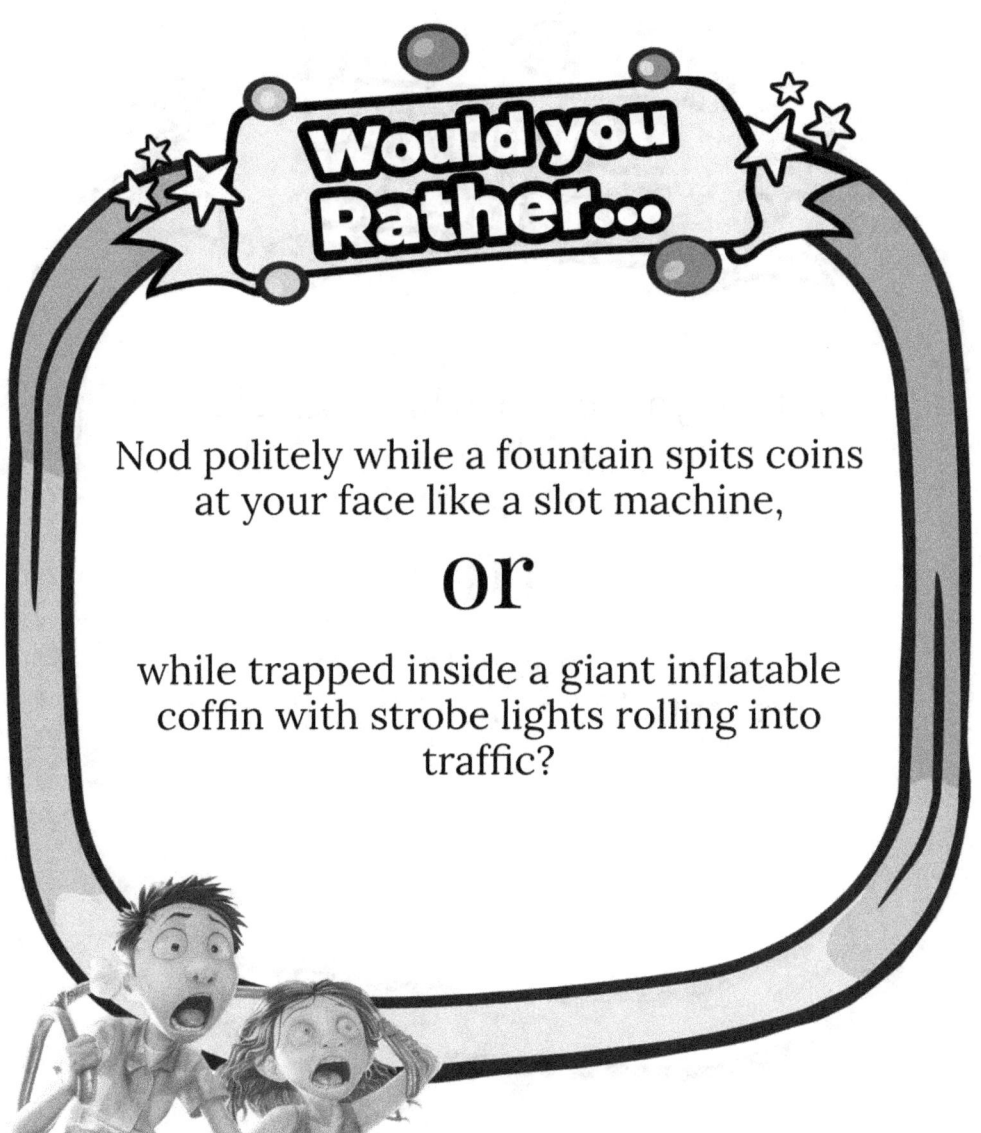

Would you Rather...

Nod politely while a fountain spits coins at your face like a slot machine,

or

while trapped inside a giant inflatable coffin with strobe lights rolling into traffic?

Reflection
Romance isn't supposed to feel like a rave or a casino.

Share It
Which awkward escape attempt would land you on TikTok first? #FirstDateWYR

Fun Fact
The largest coin fountain in the world collects over $1 million in coins annually.

Would you Rather...

Pretend you're cool while your clothes get magnetically pulled to a giant sculpture,

or

while your shoe gets permanently cemented into an art installation?

Reflection
Modern art always ruins the vibe.

Share It
Which excuse would you mumble? #FirstDateWYR

Fun Fact
In 1989, a 340-ton steel sculpture in NYC had to be dismantled after magnet issues.

Would you Rather...

Keep talking like nothing's wrong as a flock of drones follows you broadcasting "HOT DATE IN PROGRESS,"

or

as a runaway Zamboni slowly chases you down the street?

Reflection
Privacy isn't real, and neither is dignity.

Share It
Which humiliation would you pray no one filmed? #FirstDateWYR

Fun Fact
The first Zamboni ice resurfacer was invented in 1949 in California.

The Desperate Recovery Attempt | 105

Chapter 10 – The Big WTF Moment

Vibe: A single massive, surreal, or humiliating twist happens — the point where both people question if they're on a hidden camera show.

This is the turning point where hope officially flatlines.

Would you Rather...

Accidentally propose when the spotlight drops on you mid-date,

or

have a skywriter spell out "WILL YOU MARRY ME" above you even though you didn't hire them?

Reflection
Nothing like skipping 37 relationship steps in under a minute.

Share It
Which proposal disaster makes you change your name and flee the country?
#FirstDateWYR

Fun Fact
The first public skywriting in the U.S. was done in 1922 over New York City.

Would you Rather...

Have a UFO land and two aliens ask if you're their blind date,

or

a flash mob of Victorian ghost cosplayers insist you lead a séance?

Reflection
Both options scream "wrong franchise" for your love life.

Share It
Which crossover episode tanks your evening faster — Space Tinder or Regency Haunting? #FirstDateWYR

Fun Fact
The term "flying saucer" took off after pilot Kenneth Arnold's 1947 sighting.

Would you Rather...

Discover your table is actually part of a live escape room,

or

discover your seats are on stage for a surprise opera performance?

Reflection
Imagine realizing dinner was a puzzle all along.

Share It
Which reveal makes you bolt first — Appetizer Enigma or Front-Row Aria? #FirstDateWYR

Fun Fact
Modern escape rooms kicked off in Japan around 2007 before going global.

The Big WTF Moment

Would you Rather...

Have the floor open into a hidden trampoline that catapults you mid-sentence,

or

a confetti-stuffed weather balloon crash through the ceiling mid-toast?

Reflection
Nothing says romance like unintended flight.

Share It
Which airborne fiasco gets you dumped faster — Surprise Launch or Glitter Meteor? #FirstDateWYR

Fun Fact
Weather balloons typically carry radiosondes to measure temperature, humidity, and pressure.

Would you Rather...

Have your ex show up as the hired entertainment,

or

your date's ex show up as the maître d' and refuse to serve you?

Reflection
A front-row seat to unresolved drama.

Share It
Which ex encounter ruins your reputation fastest — Show Stopper or Door Stopper? #FirstDateWYR

Fun Fact
"Maître d'" is short for maître d'hôtel, French for "master of the house."

Would you Rather...

Be serenaded mid-bite by a gospel choir singing breakup songs,

or

by a heavy-metal band screaming love ballads?

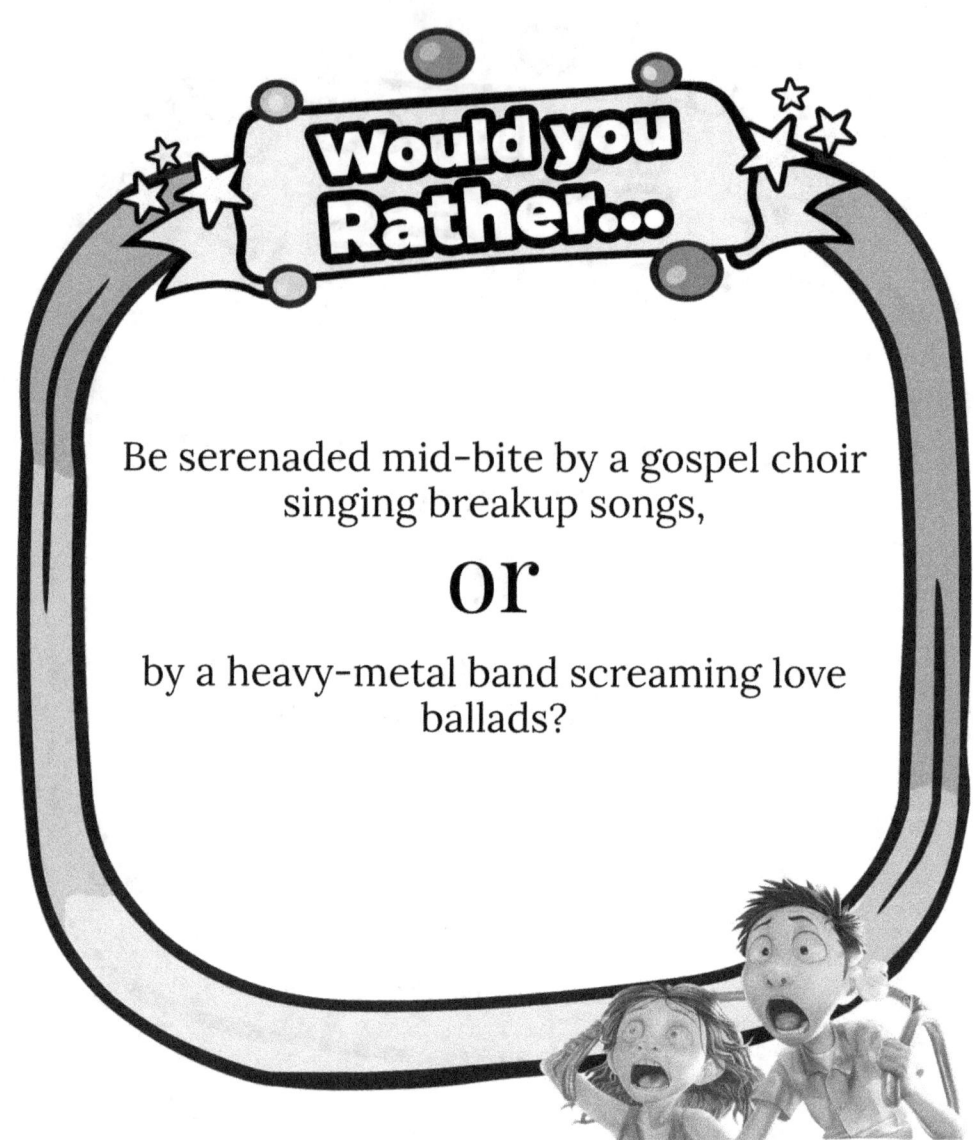

Reflection
First dates are hard enough without spit-screamed lyrics.

Share It
Which sonic ambush haunts your dreams longer — Hallelujah, We're Over or Growlmance? #FirstDateWYR

Fun Fact
Metal ballads ("power ballads") became a staple in the 1980s rock scene.

Would you Rather...

Have a ventriloquist's dummy pull up a chair to advise your date,

or

20 inflatable tube men pop up around your table with a banner that says "KISS ALREADY!"?

Reflection
Nothing sets romance back like unsolicited puppet therapy or flailing plastic hype.

Share It
Which public pressure cooker makes you fold first — Puppet Coach or Wacky-Wavy Wingmen? #FirstDateWYR

Fun Fact
"Air dancers" were popularized at the 1996 Olympics by artist Doron Gazit.

The Big WTF Moment

Would you Rather...

Have a parade of competitive cereal eaters storm the restaurant mid-meal,

or

a giant inflatable duck slowly expand between your tables until you can't see each other?

Reflection
Breakfast shouldn't have a marching section, and ducks aren't privacy screens.

Share It
Which oversized interruption kills your appetite faster — Cereal Stampede or Duck Divide? #FirstDateWYR

Fun Fact
The first ready-to-eat breakfast cereal ("Granula") was created in 1863 by James Caleb Jackson.

Would you Rather...

Be forced to deliver a surprise TED-style talk titled "Why I Deserve a Second Date,"

or

be dragged onstage to improvise a wedding toast for strangers?

Reflection
Either way, you're pitching for your life while sober.

Share It
Which mic-drop nightmare would you bomb harder — TED Beg or Toast of Shame? #FirstDateWYR

Fun Fact
TED's first conference was held in 1984, bringing together tech, entertainment, and design.

Would you Rather...

Have a gremlin crawl out of your date's backpack and loudly narrate your most embarrassing memories,

or

have a hypnotist accidentally convince you two that you're already soulmates?

Reflection
Gremlins always start with the worst chapter.

Share It
Which forced trauma bond would you survive longer — Goblin Biography or Hypno-Honeymoon? #FirstDateWYR

Fun Fact
"Gremlin" lore was popularized by British pilots in the 1920s to explain mischievous malfunctions.

Chapter 11 – The Awkward Goodbye Nobody Wanted

Vibe: Attempts to wrap things up are painfully, ridiculously weird — like gifts you can't carry or exits that make no sense.

You both know this should end, but the universe insists on squeezing in one last cringe

Would you Rather...

Say goodbye while dangling from a rented hot air balloon shaped like a miniature chihuahua,

or

while riding a horse-drawn chariot blasting techno music down Main Street?

Reflection
Nothing like an exit that makes the police wonder about your life choices.

Share It
Which exit strategy would get you cuffed faster? #FirstDateWYR

Fun Fact
The world's smallest dog ever recorded was a Chihuahua standing just 3.8 inches tall.

Would you Rather...

Say goodbye while dangling from a construction crane,

or

while being slowly lowered into the subway on a platform of helium balloons?

Reflection
Graceful exits are overrated.

Share It
Which awkward finale would trend harder on TikTok?
#FirstDateWYR

Fun Fact
The first modern crane was built in 1838 to unload ships in harbors.

The Awkward Goodbye Nobody Wanted

Would you Rather...

Accidentally hand your date your tax returns instead of your phone number,

or

hand them your Netflix password written on a subpoena?

Reflection
Nothing screams romance like unpaid fines.

Share It
Which paperwork would get you ghosted faster? #FirstDateWYR

Fun Fact
The average American household uses at least 4 streaming services.

Would you Rather...

End the night by being vacuum-sealed into a giant shrink-wrap tube,

or

by having your goodbye sky-projected onto a passing blimp in Comic Sans font?

Reflection
Romance has never looked so suffocating or tacky.

Share It
Which bizarre finale would scar you longer? #FirstDateWYR

Fun Fact
The Goodyear Blimp was designated a U.S. national landmark in 2014.

The Awkward Goodbye Nobody Wanted

Would you Rather...

Hug goodbye, but accidentally setting off an airbag,

or

handshake goodbye, but it triggers a can of whipped cream hidden in your sleeve?

Reflection
Safety features and dairy aren't sexy together.

Share It
Which malfunction would you rather survive?
#FirstDateWYR

Fun Fact
Airbags deploy in about 30 milliseconds during a crash.

Would you Rather...

Be mistaken for the mayor and dragged into a trial by fire in a medieval-style town square,

or

be mistaken for a time traveller and handed the keys to a nuclear launch silo?

Reflection
Nothing ends a date like being given world-ending responsibility.

Share It
Which case of mistaken identity would ruin your week faster? #FirstDateWYR

Fun Fact
The concept of trial by fire was practiced in medieval Europe as a test of guilt or innocence.

Would you Rather...

Try to bow politely and accidentally trigger a trap door into a slide that dumps you three blocks away,

or

try to curtsy and activate sprinklers that rain down neon paint?

Reflection
Either way, subtlety has left the chat.

Share It
Which farewell would you rather trend for? #FirstDateWYR

Fun Fact
Neon paints glow under blacklight due to fluorescent pigments.

The Awkward Goodbye Nobody Wanted

Would you Rather...

Have the goodbye kiss interrupted by an army of robots chanting your Tinder bio,

or

by a hologram of your ex hosting a live auction of your childhood stuffed animals?

Reflection
Nothing crushes romance like watching your teddy bear get sold to a stranger.

Share It
Which public humiliation would you rage-quit over first? #FirstDateWYR

Fun Fact
The world's most expensive teddy bear, a Steiff Louis Vuitton, sold for over $2 million.

The Awkward Goodbye Nobody Wanted

Would you Rather...

Get your coat back, only to find it's filled with wet cement,

or

get your shoes back to discover they've been welded together?

Reflection
Fashion shouldn't require power tools.

Share It
Which sabotaged wardrobe would ruin your commute? #FirstDateWYR

Fun Fact
Cement hardens within 10 minutes of mixing with water.

Would you Rather...

Say goodnight, only for a billboard across the street to light up with "MARRY ME, STRANGER,"

or

for a drone swarm above you to glitch and spell your name wrong in giant glowing letters?

Reflection
Romance is hard when technology gets drunk.

Share It
Which public stunt would you sue someone over first?
#FirstDateWYR

Fun Fact
In 2020, 1,500 drones formed a light show over Shanghai, creating animated patterns in the sky.

The Awkward Goodbye Nobody Wanted

Chapter 12 – The Ride Home Disaster Parade

Vibe: Leaving should be the easy part, but instead it turns into a final act of surreal chaos that makes you wonder if you'll ever date again.

The curtain closes, not with romance... but with a flaming clown car of shame.

Would you Rather...

Head home in a hearse blasting bubblegum pop at full volume,

or

in a school bus filled with mannequins all wearing your date's face?

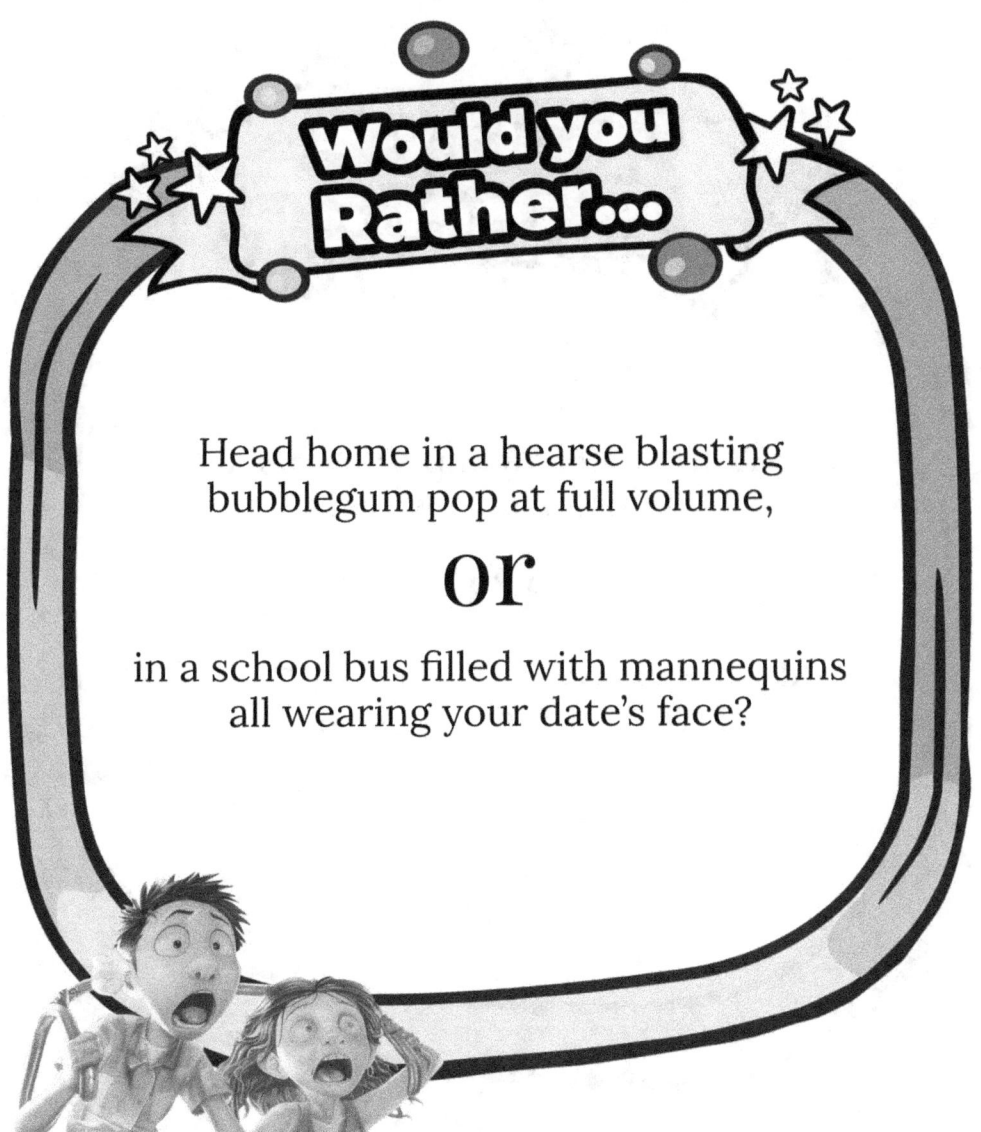

Reflection
Nothing like upbeat music and dead-eyed stares to cap off romance.

Share It
Which nightmare commute would you survive without crying? #FirstDateWYR

Fun Fact
The first motorized hearses appeared in the U.S. around 1909.

The Ride Home Disaster Parade

Would you Rather...

Ride home inside a supersized six-foot deli sub with wheels,

or

inside a hollowed-out rotary phone that rattles with every pothole?

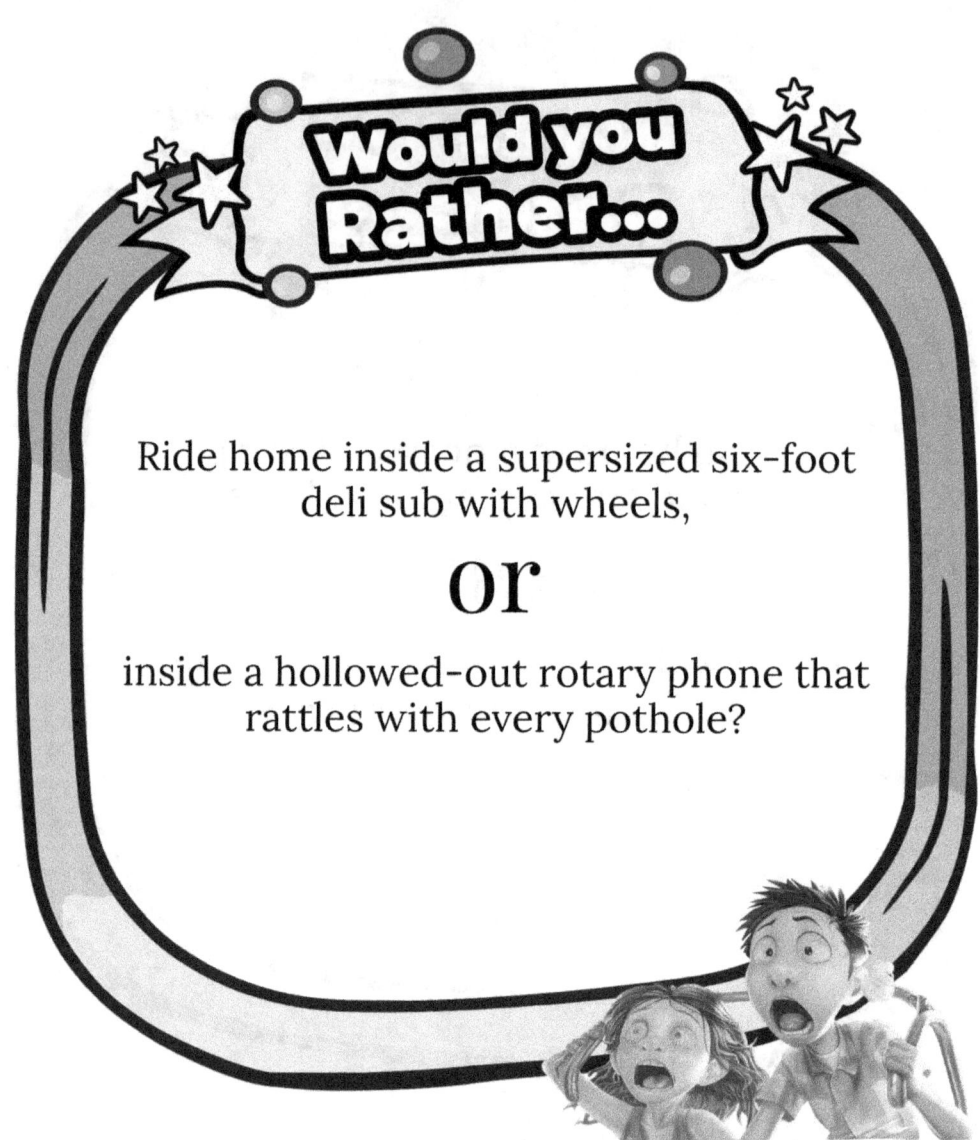

Reflection
Romance ends best when carbs and bad design collide.

Share It
Which oversized prop would you rather file an insurance claim for? #FirstDateWYR

Fun Fact
The world's longest sandwich was over 3,300 feet long, made in Italy in 2004.

Would you Rather...

Get chauffeured by a driver wearing only a cardboard cutout of the Venus de Milo,

or

by someone in a clam shell car that honks like a foghorn?

Reflection
Nothing like ancient art or seafood cosplay to ruin Uber ratings.

Share It
Which absurd chauffeur would make you delete your dating apps? #FirstDateWYR

Fun Fact
The Venus de Milo statue was discovered in 1820 on the Greek island of Milos.

The Ride Home Disaster Parade

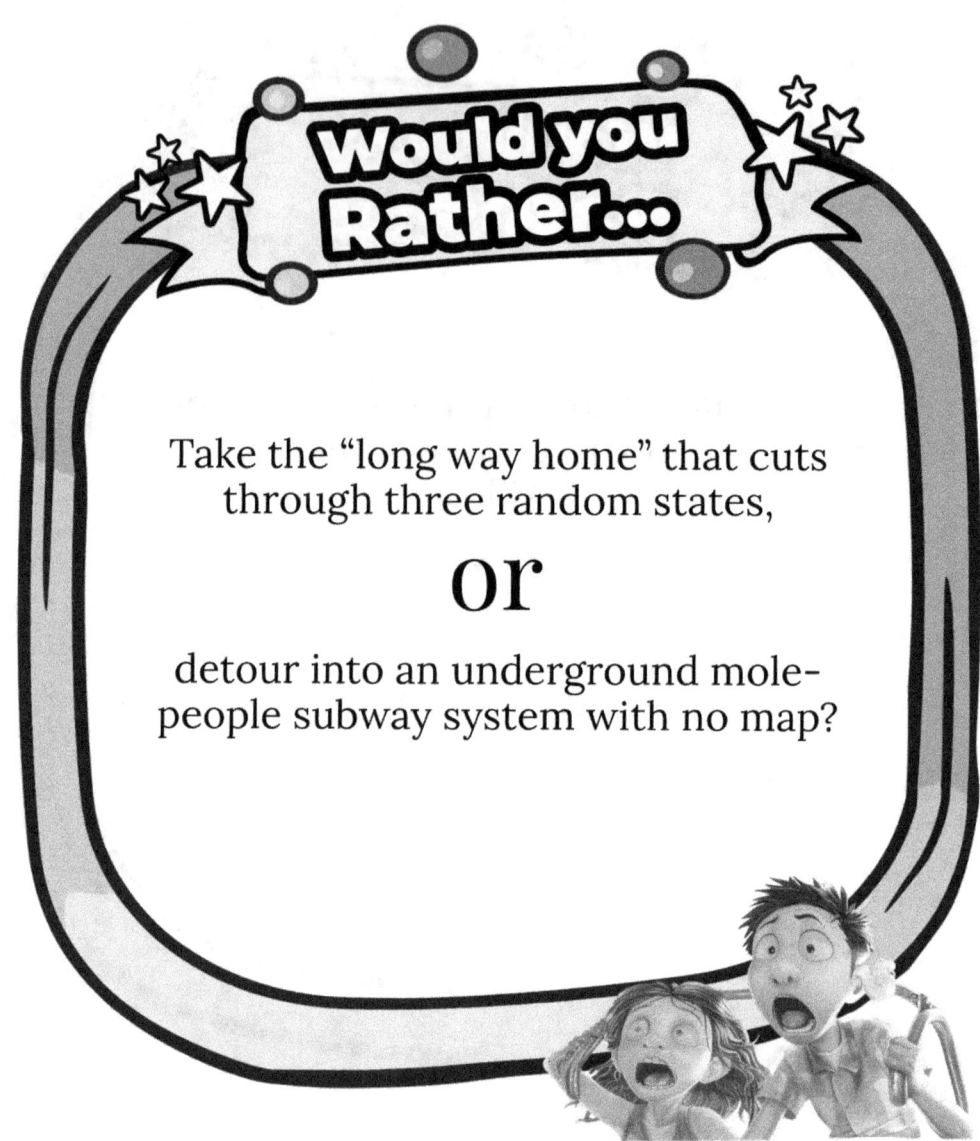

Would you Rather...

Take the "long way home" that cuts through three random states,

or

detour into an underground mole-people subway system with no map?

Reflection
Suddenly, "Are we there yet?" becomes a survival question.

Share It
Which endless detour would make you cry into your GPS first? #FirstDateWYR

Fun Fact
The longest continuous road trip route in the U.S. covers nearly 13,000 miles.

Would you Rather...

Be given a piggyback ride home by the Hunchback of Notre Dame,

or

be carried bridal-style by twelve synchronized mimes?

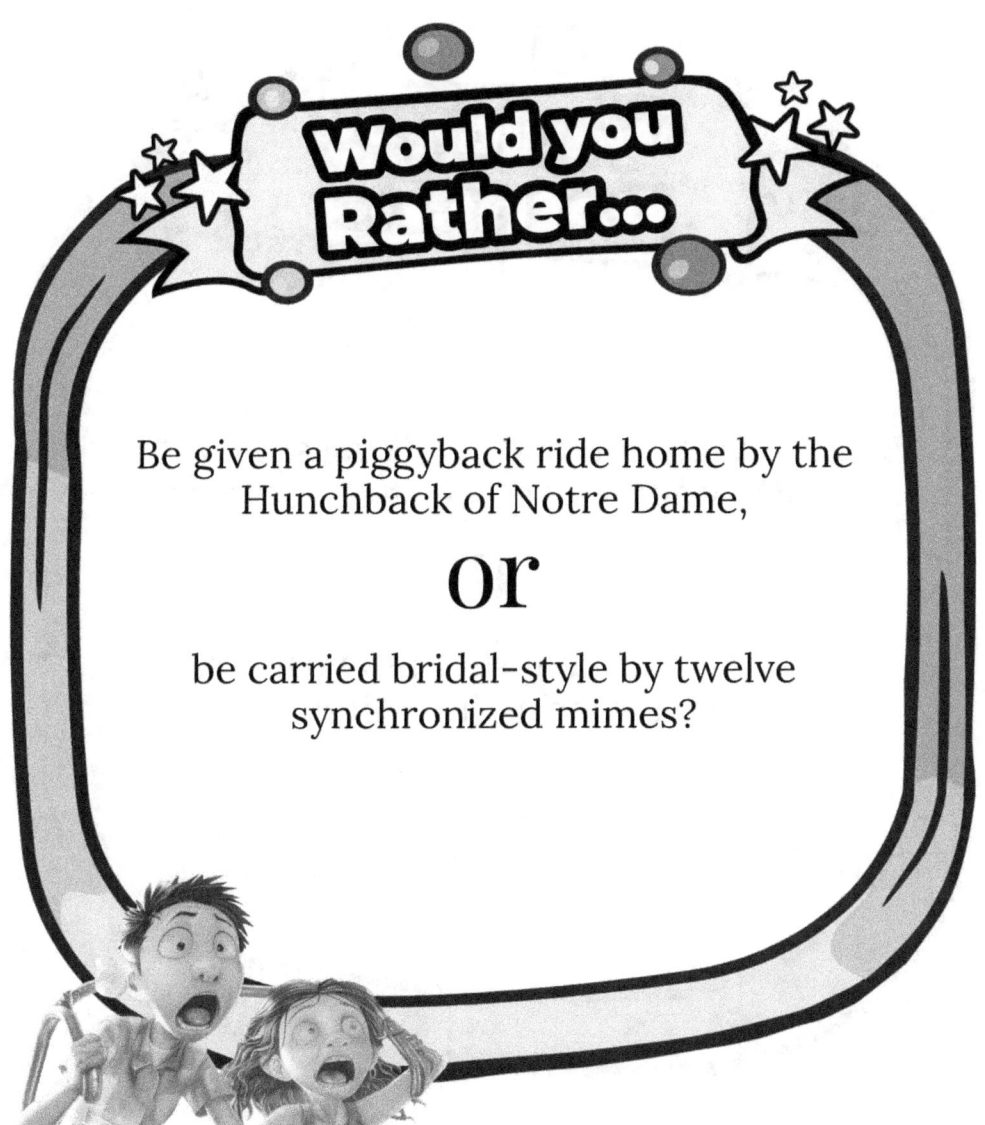

Reflection
Comfort is officially dead; only performance art remains.

Share It
Which physical escort would break you faster? #FirstDateWYR

Fun Fact
Victor Hugo's The Hunchback of Notre Dame was published in 1831.

The Ride Home Disaster Parade | 133

Would you Rather...

Get driven home by a talking snail with a heavy accent you can't understand,

or

by a self-driving shopping cart that keeps veering into ditches?

Reflection
Neither will get you there this decade, but both will test your patience.

Share It
Which chaotic ride would you livestream? #FirstDateWYR

Fun Fact
The giant African land snail can grow up to 8 inches long.

Would you Rather...

Arrive home strapped to the top of a moving carnival ride,

or

inside a fish tank sloshing with goldfish every time the brakes hit?

Reflection
You either scream or swim your way into the night.

Share It
Which ride would you rather explain to your neighbors?
#FirstDateWYR

Fun Fact
The world's tallest carnival ride swing is over 450 feet high.

The Ride Home Disaster Parade

Would you Rather...

Be dropped at your door on a magic carpet piloted by a Shakespearean actor quoting Hamlet,

or

inside a bathtub dragged by stray shopping carts?

Reflection
Fairytales and scrapyards both end in regret.

Share It
Which "vehicle" would ruin your reputation forever? #FirstDateWYR

Fun Fact
Magic carpet myths appear in Middle Eastern folklore, especially One Thousand and One Nights.

Would you Rather...

Share a ride with a squeaky rubber dog toy driving a bread-shaped car,

or

a mime piloting a hoverboard convoy while juggling pineapples?

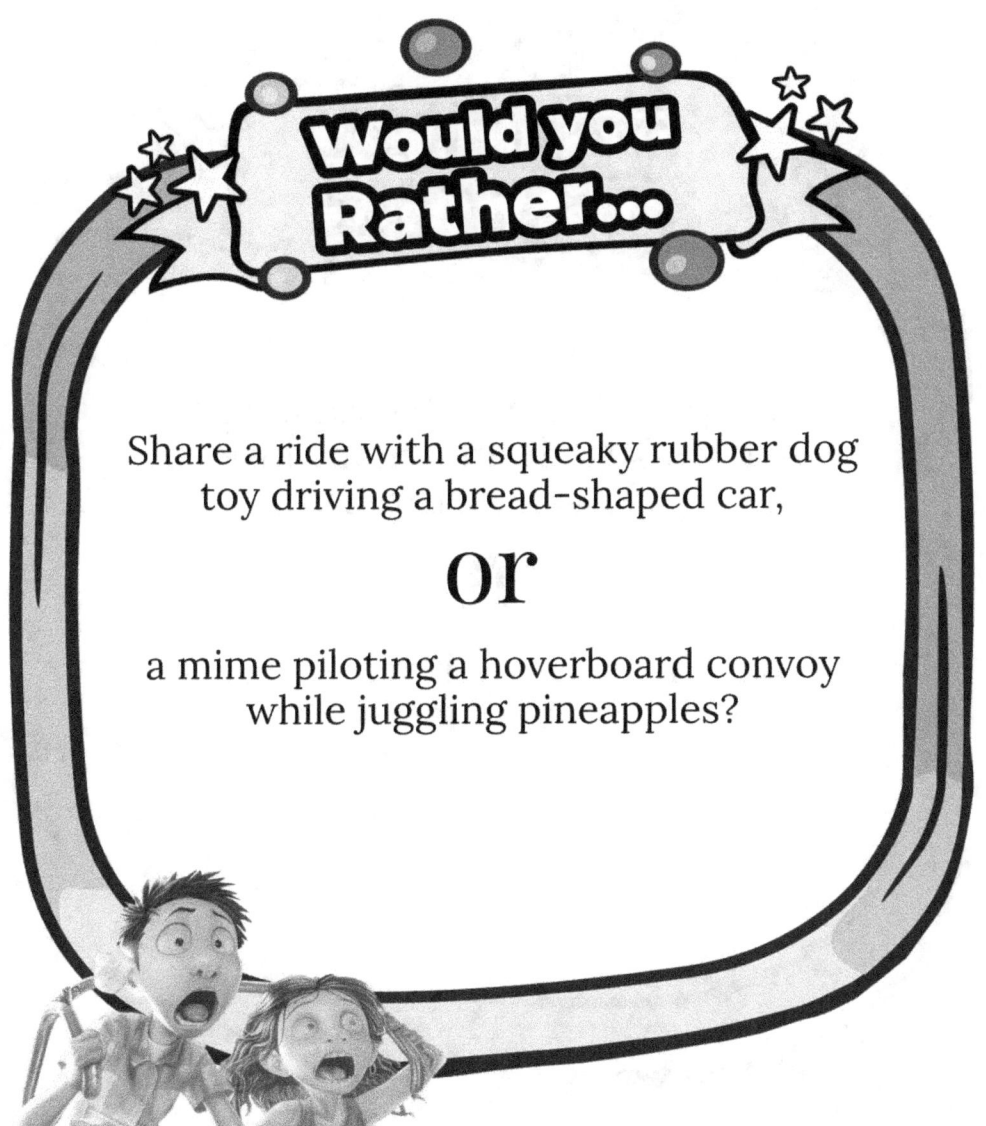

Reflection
Nothing says "safety hazard" like carbs or fruit mid-flight.

Share It
Which ridiculous transport would get you banned from the road? #FirstDateWYR

Fun Fact
The largest loaf of bread ever baked weighed over 3,400 lbs.

The Ride Home Disaster Parade

Would you Rather...

Have your final goodbye sabotaged when you're delivered home inside a giant jack-in-the-box,

or

on a float shaped like a melting popsicle?

Reflection
Either way, the neighbors will talk forever.

Share It
Which spectacle would end your dating career immediately? #FirstDateWYR

Fun Fact
The largest jack-in-the-box toy ever built measured 23 feet tall.

Reader's Challenge

Think you can come up with a Would You Rather question so absurd it would make even this book blush? We want to see it. Post your wildest creations online with #FirstDateWYR and throw them into the ring.

The most ridiculous, creative, and flat-out unhinged ones may just find their way into a future book. (Yes, that means if you once dreamed of being immortalized for asking whether you'd rather kiss goodnight through a scuba mask or on a trampoline covered in cheese slices, this is your chance.)

Final Laugh

Before you go, here's one last scenario that didn't quite fit anywhere else:

End the night by vanishing through a trap door into a medieval sewer system, or by being airlifted out by a helicopter that immediately loses your luggage over the city?

There are no right answers. Only stories your friends will never stop retelling.

And just to be clear: if you actually attempt any of these goodbyes, you're fully responsible for bail money, medical bills, and explaining things to your boss on Monday.

Acknowledgments

Dating today feels like running an obstacle course blindfolded—except the prize at the end is usually an awkward hug and a receipt you didn't want to split. This book wouldn't exist without the collective chaos of every bad pick-up line, every too-long pause, and every moment that made you think, "Wow... this is my life now." To all the brave souls who keep putting themselves out there anyway—this one's for you.

Keep the Book Going by Sharing

This book isn't meant to die quietly on your nightstand. Share it. Bring it to parties. Throw it at your friends (gently). Argue loudly over the questions and then post your battles online with #FirstDateWYR so we can all witness the chaos. The more ridiculous the debate, the better

A Thank You Note from Lewis

Thank you for picking up this book instead of pretending to text during your actual date. Thank you for laughing, rolling your eyes, and maybe questioning my sanity. Without readers like you, this book would just be me shouting absurd "what ifs" into the void—so really, you've saved me from myself.

About the Author

Lewis Mabee has made a career out of watching how people interact—sometimes sweet, sometimes strange, and often unintentionally hilarious. As a life coach and constant observer of human behavior, he's seen enough first impressions to know they rarely go the way anyone planned. When he's not turning awkward moments into comedy gold, Lewis enjoys time with family and friends, and perfecting the fine art of people-watching without getting caught.

www.ingramcontent.com/pod-product-compliance
Lightning Source LLC
Chambersburg PA
CBHW050329010526
44119CB00050B/727